In the Footsteps of John Knox

A Man of Fearless Faith

Andy Kuo

"In the Footsteps of ..." Reformation Series

© 2016 Andy Kuo
All rights reserved.

Luke Publishing
Richmond BC Canada

Front Cover Photos: Street in Geneva (author's own photo); Statue of Knox in Knox Place, Haddington (© Kim Traynor / CC BY-SA 3.0.).

Back Cover Photo: Night scene in Geneva (author's own photo).

Although the author and publisher have made every effort to provide accurate information, they are not responsible for any implications from the use of this book or for any information listed in this book.

Copyright © 2016 Andy Kuo

Library and Archives Canada Cataloguing in Publication

Kuo, Andy, author
     In the footsteps of John Knox : a man of fearless faith / Andy Kuo.

("In the footsteps of ..." reformation series)
Includes bibliographical references.
ISBN 978-0-9958266-0-1 (softcover).--ISBN 978-0-9958266-1-8 (hardcover)

     1. Knox, John, approximately 1514-1572. 2. Knox, John, approximately 1514-1572--Travel--Europe. 3. Presbyterians--Scotland--Biography. 4. Theologians--Scotland--Biography. 5. Presbyterianism. 6. Europe--Description and travel. 7. Reformation--Scotland. 8. Scotland--Church history--16th century. 9. Bible. English Geneva. I. Title. II. Series: "In the footsteps of ..." reformation series

BX9223.K86 2016   285'.2092   C2016-907651-2

A catalogue record for this book is available from Library and Archives Canada.

Books in the Series

In the Footsteps of John Knox

In the Footsteps of Martin Luther

About the Author

Andy Kuo is an ordained minister of the Presbyterian Church in Canada. His research interests include church history and theology. In his leisure time, he enjoys traveling to historical places.

Dedicated to my wife Julie and my parents.

Contents

Foreword	*ii*
Preface	*iii*
Timeline	*v*
Chapter 1: Formative Years	**1**
Travel: Haddington	4
Chapter 2: From a Catholic Priest to a Galley Slave	**9**
Travel: St Andrews	13
Chapter 3: Exile in England (1547–1554)	**23**
Travel: England	28
Chapter 4: Frankfurt	**35**
Travel: Dieppe and Frankfurt	41
Chapter 5: The Most Perfect School of Christ	**44**
Travel: Geneva, Switzerland	48
Chapter 6: Back to Scotland	**55**
Travel: Perth	62
Chapter 7: Mary, Queen of Scots	**64**
Travel: Stirling	69
Chapter 8: Knox's Final Years	**73**
Travel: Edinburgh	77
Bibliography	*85*
Copyright and Credits	*86*
About the Book	*87*

Foreword

John Knox's presence in parts of Scotland does not surprise us. When one stumbles across the statue of him in St. Giles, or stands beneath the towering statue at New College, or walks past John Knox house on the Royal Mile, one is not surprised. But John Knox was shaped, not only by Scotland, but by his experiences in England, as well as on the continent in Dieppe, Frankfurt and Geneva.

Andy Kuo weaves together Knox's life with the various places he lived or where key events in his life occurred. The story of Knox's life unfolds as the book moves from place to place, and invites the reader on each stop to look around and experience the particular location. One can indeed, follow in the footsteps of Knox.

Other readers may be more interested in the history and use the book as a guide to the particular part of Scotland or Europe in which they find themselves. In Geneva, one can see the sites as well as place that moment in Knox's life into the broader context of his life. In St Andrews, one can visit the church where he preached his first sermon, as well as the Castle in which he lived, and from where he was taken to the French Galley's after the fall of that Castle.

However one approaches this book, one will leave it knowing more about John Knox, his times, and the places he influenced and which influenced him. It will be a fascinating and worthwhile journey.

Dr. Stuart Macdonald
Professor of Church and Society
Knox College, Toronto School of Theology

Preface

John Knox, Scotland's great sixteenth-century reformer, was a man of fearless faith. Born in Haddington, Knox studied at St Andrews University and was ordained into the priesthood in 1536. He came under the influence of Protestant thought in the 1540s, was drawn to Protestant preacher George Wishart, and became his follower. After Wishart was arrested and burned at the stake, Knox went into hiding. He eventually joined the Protestant forces who were besieged at St Andrews Castle in 1547. When the castle was taken by the French, he was forced to become a French galley slave. Nineteen months later, he was released. He went into exile in England and served in different ministerial capacities, including as a chaplain in King Edward VI's court.

When Catholic queen Mary Tudor came to the throne in England, Knox fled to continental Europe, where he eventually became one of the pastors of the English exile congregation in Geneva. Together with other English exiles, they completed the translation of the first English Bible with verse numbers and annotated commentary, known as the Geneva Bible. In 1559, he returned to Scotland to participate in Scotland's Reformation. Knox's passion, zeal, and deep trust in God helped transform Scotland into a Protestant nation. He served as the minister at St Giles' Cathedral in Edinburgh in the 1560s until his death in 1572.

In this book, I would like to take you on a journey that will explore the key moments of the life of John Knox, discover his faith and follow his footsteps to places where he traveled. In eight chapters, we will encounter the important stages in Knox's life and ministry. At the end of each chapter, a travel section will introduce you to the cities and sites where he traveled and where key events transpired in his life.

It is my hope that this book will help you to gain knowledge of the life of Scotland's "Great Reformer," to follow Knox's footsteps to places that he visited, and more importantly, to gain insights into how his faith shaped him and the people around him.

Andy Kuo
Toronto, Canada

Knox's Europe
Modified from the original work by Joostik / CC BY-SA 3.0

Timeline

Formative Years

ca. 1514–15	Born in Haddington, East Lothian, Scotland.
ca. 1529–30	Left Haddington and entered St Andrews University.
1536	Graduated from University of St Andrews and was ordained as a priest.
1540	Became a notary apostolic.
1543	Converted to Protestantism.
1545	Became the bodyguard to Protestant preacher George Wishart.
1546	Wishart martyred. Protestants at St Andrews Castle fall under siege.
1547	Joined the Protestants in the castle. Preached his first Protestant sermon. Protestants in the castle surrendered to the French.
1547-49	Imprisoned as a slave in a French galley.

Exile Years

1549	Began pastoring in Berwick-upon-Tweed in northern England.
1550	Met Elizabeth Bowes and her daughter Marjorie.
1551	Moved to Newcastle.
1552	Preached at King Edward VI's court. Disputed practice of kneeling at Communion. Betrothed to Marjorie Bowes.

1553	Forced into hiding when Catholic Queen Mary Tudor came to the throne. Exile in continental Europe.
1554	Became pastor of the English congregation in Frankfurt.
1555/6	Returned to Scotland secretly. Married Marjorie Bowes.
1556	Became one of the English pastors of the English exile congregation in Geneva.
1557	Planned to return to Scotland at the invitation of Protestant nobles but was stopped at Dieppe. Knox's first son, Nathaniel, was born.
1558	Wrote *The First Blast of the Trumpet against the Monstrous Regiment of Women*, *The Appellation to the Nobility*, and *The Letter to the Commonalty*, supporting active resistance against idolatrous rulers. Birth of his second son, Eleazer.

Return to Scotland

1559	Back to Scotland. Preached a sermon condemning idolatry at St John's Kirk, Perth, that led to rebellion. Selected as the minister at St Giles' Church, Edinburgh.
1560	Parliament passed series of laws implementing Protestantism. Knox's wife, Marjorie, died.
1561	Knox helped to write the *First Book of Discipline*. Mary, Queen of Scots, returned to Scotland. Knox summoned by Mary, Queen of Scots.
1564	Remarried to Margaret Stewart.
1571	Left Edinburgh due to civil war; traveled to St Andrews.
1572	Returned to Edinburgh. Died in Edinburgh and was buried at St Giles' Church.

Chapter 1: Formative Years

John Knox was born in 1514 or 1515 in Haddington, a burgh (autonomous town) located on the banks of the River Tyne in the fertile valley of East Lothian. Little is known about Knox's childhood. Even his year of birth is uncertain. At the time of Knox's birth, his family lived on Giffordgate, a narrow street on the east side of the River Tyne. On the far end of the street was a stone bridge that led to the town. Across the River Tyne stood the parish church of St Mary's, where Knox was baptized as an infant.

As Knox was not the eldest son in the family, he was unable to inherit his father's merchant business. He had to seek his vocation elsewhere. At that time, a career in the church would have been the best opportunity for him, as the church was the largest institution in Scotland. It would also help the Knox family to climb up the social ladder. Thus, in addition to his own passion for the church, Knox was likely encouraged by his family to pursue a religious career.

When he grew old enough, Knox's family sent him to the song school attached to St Mary's church.[1] This marked the beginning of his formal education. At the school, he learned to read and sing using liturgical books. It was here that he learned the daily routine of services, especially the singing of the Psalms. This left a permanent mark on his heart. Even on his deathbed, he recalled the numbering of the Psalms not from the Protestant Bible but from a slightly different numbering system used by the Roman Catholics.[2]

After learning the basics of singing and reading at the song school,

---

1 Jane E. A. Dawson, *John Knox* (New Haven: Yale University Press, 2015), 15.
2 On his deathbed, Knox spoke of Psalm 9 when referring to a passage in Psalm 10 in the Protestant Bible. John Knox, *The Works of John Knox*, ed. Laing David (Edinburgh: James Thin, 1895), I:638.

Knox moved on to study arts curriculum at the grammar school in Haddington. While studying there, he also learned Latin. His studies involved a method called "double translation," in which the student would translate a passage from Latin to English and then translate it from English to Latin again. It was at this stage of his life that he became familiar with the Vulgate Bible, the Latin edition of the Bible used by Roman Catholics. This Bible became so familiar to him that later in his adult life, whenever he thought of Bible verses, the passages from the Vulgate Bible were the ones that came to his mind.

Studied at St Andrews University

When Knox was about fifteen years old, he left Haddington and traveled to Scotland's ancient ecclesiastical capital, St Andrews. He was to enroll in St Andrews University, the oldest university in Scotland. He was set to study at St Salvator's College, the divinity school at St Andrews University, to prepare for a career in the priesthood.

At St Andrews, he learned how to carefully study texts; he enjoyed arguments and debates. He also loved words and language. Perhaps it was in these formative years that he developed his oratory skills, which greatly helped him in his later years of preaching and promoting the Reformation in Scotland.

Unlike many other European universities, where humanism became the primary teaching method and curriculum, Scotland at the time was still in the traditional scholastic camp. Knox likely was taught by the renowned scholastic scholar John Mair, who had returned to Scotland after a distinguished career at the University of Paris. Mair also came from East Lothian, the county where Knox was born. Knox was attracted to Mair's teaching and was proud to study under him.[3]

Mair was highly critical of the corruption of the Roman Catholic Church. He also insisted that even though monarchs were chosen by God, their authority came from the people.[4] Although Knox remained a Roman Catholic during his years of study, Mair's radical thought was an eye-opener, and he would continue to ponder these thoughts in years to come. Years later, even after Knox's conversion to Protestantism, he still pondered the relationship between the monarchy and the people. More specifically, he would wonder whether ordinary people had the right to resist idolatry.

---

3 Ibid., I:xix.
4 Rosalind K. Marshall, *John Knox* (Edinburgh: Birlinn, 2008), chap. 1.

Ordained into Priesthood

In 1536, Knox was ordained in Edinburgh and thus earned the title of Sir John Knox, a courtesy title given to priests. However, it was difficult to obtain a position in a parish. Out of Scotland's population of three hundred thousand, it is estimated that there were more than three thousand priests, so there were simply more priests than posts. By 1540, Knox was able to secure employment as a notary apostolic, equivalent to a country lawyer today. In Knox's time, the position remained under church jurisdiction. He moved back to his childhood home, Haddington, where he lived comfortably until things changed in 1542.

Some Facts about Pre-Reformation Churches in Scotland

The Church of Scotland was the wealthiest institution in the country before the dawn of the Reformation. The Church's income was £400,000 per annum, compared to the crown's income of around 40,000 per annum.[5] Most of the money went to religious houses, cathedrals, and universities. Church offices often remained in the hands of nobles and were passed down from one generation to another. For example, King James V had five of his illegitimate sons appointed to positions in the church.

***

In the travel section that follows, we will visit Knox's hometown of Haddington on the banks of the River Tyne. We will see the magnificent parish church of St Mary's, where Knox was baptized, the quiet street where the Knox family resided, and the grammar school that Knox attended. The seaside town of St Andrews will be introduced in the travel section after chapter 2.

---

5 Ibid.

Travel: Haddington

Haddington is a burgh located on the banks of the River Tyne in the fertile valley of East Lothian. The town is twenty miles east of Scotland's capital city, Edinburgh. Knox was proud of his Haddington roots. In 1566, when Knox was in his fifties, he looked back at his hometown with pride. This town produced men of "wisdom and ability," including Walter Bower, the author of *Scotichronicon*, and John Mair, the famous professor who taught Knox when Knox was studying at St Andrews.[6]

Haddington, East Lothian
© Jonathan Odenbuck / CC BY-SA 3.0.

The burgh's strategic location meant that it often lay on the route of invasion from England in the south. Life in East Lothian was often disturbed by war, from medieval times through the sixteenth century. By Knox's time, there had been several invasions. The Anglo-Scottish war in the 1540s, known as the "Rough Wooings," caused serious destruction to the town, including damage to the town's parish church, St Mary's.

---

6 Quoted in Dawson, *John Knox*, 13.

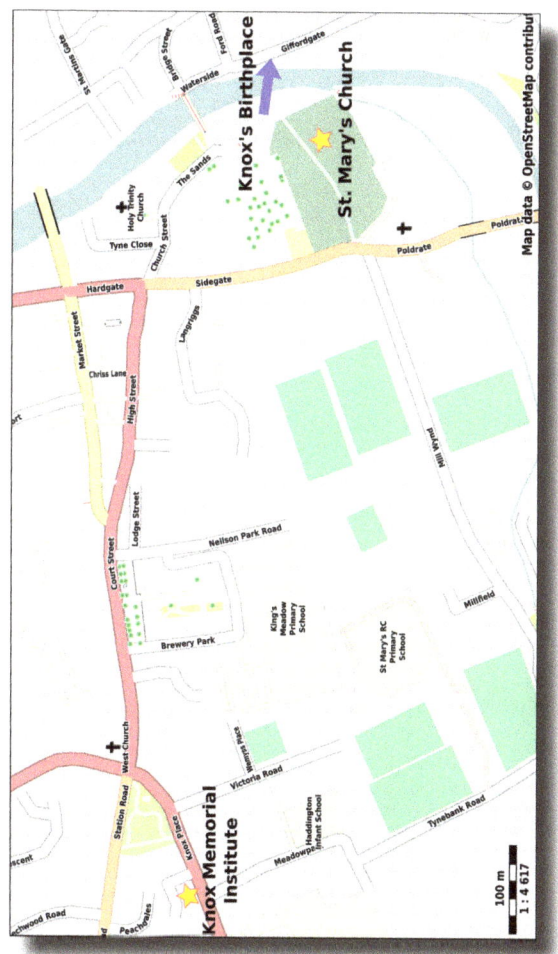

Map of Haddington

St Mary's Church

Known as "the lamp of Lothian," St Mary's parish church was the largest parish church in Scotland. This long gray-and-red sandstone Gothic building has an interior space larger than that of Scotland's famous St Giles' Church in Edinburgh. Its exterior length is 62.8 m, which is 0.7 m longer than St Giles'. St Mary's square tower is ninety feet high.

St Mary's Church, Haddington
© Kim Traynor / CC BY-SA 3.0.

When Protestant preacher George Wishart started his preaching tour in Scotland, Knox was drawn to him and became his bodyguard. Wishart came to preach in St Mary's in January of 1547, and Knox accompanied him, standing below the pulpit bearing a two-handed sword. During the service, Wishart warned the people to turn away from the corrupt Roman Catholic Church; otherwise, the town would be plagued by fire and sword and would be occupied by foreigners.

Knox saw Wishart's prophetic vision realized when the English invaded Scotland and besieged Haddington in 1548. The war left much of Haddington ruined. St Mary's roof was destroyed. In 1561, on Knox's advice, the church added a wall at the east end of the nave so that the nave, at least, could be used again. For the next several hundred years, the tower, transepts, and choir area remained uncovered, with no roof to protect them. It was not until 1973 that the roof was completely restored.

Interior of St Mary's Church, Haddington
© Otter / CC BY-SA 3.0.

No records exist of Knox ever preaching at St Mary's, but it is likely that he did, since the inventory of his estate lists a pension from the church in Haddington.

John Knox's Birthplace

During Knox's childhood, he and his family lived on Giffordgate Street on the east side of the River Tyne. The exact location of the Knox family's residence is uncertain. On this street, there is a stone bearing the inscription: "Near this spot stood the house in which was born John Knox AD 1505. In commemoration an oak tree was here planted 29th March 1881 after the wish of the late Thomas Carlyle."

Plaque that marks Knox's birthplace
© Becky Williamson / CC BY-SA 2.0.

The stone was laid in 1881, based on the fact that a family by the name of Knox once lived in a house near the stone. However, records suggest that that family did not move in until a few years after John Knox's death in 1572. The birth year is likely also incorrect, as contemporary historians believe that he was born either in 1514 or 1515.

Knox Memorial Institute

Knox Memorial Institute, now known as Knox Place, was located where John Knox attended grammar school in Haddington. The existing building was erected in 1879 to replace the famous old school. To commemorate Scotland's "Great Reformer," a full-size statue of John Knox wielding the Bible was erected at a cost of £10,000. Since then, the school has moved, and the building, now called Knox Place, has been converted into a home for the elderly.

Statue of John Knox at Knox Place
© Kim Traynor / CC BY-SA 3.0.

Chapter 2: From a Catholic Priest to a Galley Slave

The political backdrop changed dramatically in the 1540s. In November of 1542, shortly after Scotland's King James V's army was defeated by King Henry VIII of England, James V died and left his six-day-old daughter Mary, Queen of Scots to succeed to the throne. The Second Earl of Arran was soon appointed as regent to rule the country. Fearing that Henry VIII's army would invade Scotland in this political vacuum, Arran quickly made peace with England, agreeing that the infant queen would marry Henry VIII's son, Prince Edward.

Since England had adopted Protestantism under King Henry VIII's reign, the new regent also encouraged the spread of Protestantism in Scotland. He sent two Protestant preachers, Thomas Guillaume and John Rough, across the country on a preaching tour. In addition, Arran permitted the distribution of the English Bible. However, this shift toward Protestantism was short-lived. Arran's cousin, Archbishop David Beaton, urged Arran to break with England and align with Scotland's traditional ally, France.

Encountered George Wishart

While the two Protestant preachers were traveling and preaching around Scotland, Knox happened to hear both of them. We do not know how much influence they had on Knox, as he did not write about it, nor did he write about his conversion from Roman Catholicism to Protestantism. If these two preachers sowed the seeds of Protestantism in Knox's head, then George Wishart was the one who kindled the fire in his heart.

Wishart returned to Scotland in 1543 after spending five years in exile in Switzerland, Germany, and England. His charismatic preaching style, urging church reform, had drawn many followers. On December 13, 1543, Knox heard a sermon preached by Wishart in Leith. Hearing Wishart preach on the image of the sheep following Christ as the Shepherd from John's Gospel, Knox experienced a personal call to follow the Shepherd's voice.

Drawn to Wishart's message, he soon became Wishart's disciple. For Knox, Wishart was both hero and role model, and he referred to him as "Master George." To remain close to Wishart, he even invented a new role for himself, the bodyguard of his master, and he carried a sword as he accompanied Wishart on his preaching tour in Scotland.

When Scotland's alliance with England came to an end in 1545, the nation quickly shifted back to its traditional ally, France. The shift in foreign policy meant that any efforts toward church reform were short-lived. It was also becoming dangerous for those who promoted Protestantism in Scotland. As Wishart traveled and preached, he was discouraged by frequent dismissals. In January of 1546, Knox accompanied him to Knox's hometown, Haddington, where Wishart preached at St Mary's church. As Wishart preached, he warned the people that if they remained lukewarm, the town would be plagued by fire and the sword and would be occupied by foreigners. Wishart's prophecy was fulfilled when English invaders destroyed Haddington and set the parish on fire. Later on, as Knox saw his home town burst into flame, he took the words of Wishart to heart and was even more firmly resolved to carry out the Reformation in Scotland.

On the day after Wishart preached that prophetic sermon, sensing that his arrest was near, he told Knox not to follow him. He said, "Return you to your bairns…one is sufficient for a sacrifice."[7] Knox protested but eventually obeyed, and on that very night, after singing Psalm 51 ("Have mercy on me now, good Lord"), Wishart was arrested and transferred to Archbishop Beaton's residence at St Andrews Castle. He was burned at the stake on March 1, 1546. Knox went into hiding, moving from house to house for his safety's sake.

The Siege of St Andrews Castle

Wishart's death did not put an end to the Reformation movement in Scotland. On May 29, 1546, Protestants in Fife plotting vengeance waited outside St Andrews Castle. In the early morning, around five

---

7 Ibid.

o'clock, when the tower bridge was lowered and the gate was opened, they rushed into the castle. They ran to Cardinal Beaton's room and stabbed him to death, then barricaded themselves in the castle.

Hearing of the murder of Archbishop Beaton, Scotland's Privy Council met; there were different opinions, but it was decided to besiege the castle. An attempt to capture the castle by undermining was successfully defended by the Protestants digging a counter-mine. Since the council was divided, there was no strong attempt to capture the castle, and people remained free to come and go from it. The siege continued until the summer of the following year, during which the Protestants inside requested reinforcements from England. On the other hand, the queen's mother, Mary of Guise—a devout French Roman Catholic—sought support from France in an attempt to capture the castle and the Protestant rebels inside.

On Easter of 1547, Knox joined the Protestants under siege, teaching the boys in the castle about the Gospel of John. His teaching and preaching capabilities were soon recognized. Protestant leaders John Rough and Henry Balnaves urged him to take up the task of becoming preacher for the castle. He refused their proposal, unsure whether this was really God's calling. However, Rough and Balnaves did not give up. Rough even said, "Ye shall not be offended, albeit that I speak unto you that which I have in charge, even from all those that are here present which is this. In the name of God and of his son Jesus Christ, and in the name of these that presently calls you by my mouth, I charge you that ye refuse not this holy vocation."[8] Knox burst into tears and went back to his chambers. After a week to pray and discern God's calling, he finally accepted.

The following Sunday, he preached his first sermon on Daniel 7 reflecting on the struggle of the true Church. Later in his life, when he reflected upon this calling, he wrote, "How small was my learning, and how weak I was of judgment, when Jesus Christ called me to be his steward."[9]

Meanwhile, the siege continued. The Protestants refused to surrender, betting their hope on English reinforcement. On June 29, 1547, a fleet was finally spotted. The Protestants rejoiced at first but soon realized that it was not the reinforcement they had been waiting for.

---

8 Ibid., I:187.
9 Ibid., III:269.

Instead, it was the French army (on the pleas of Mary of Guise). They landed in the city on July 24, 1547, dragged their cannons through the streets and positioned them on top of the Priory Church and St Salvator's College. At four o'clock on the morning of July 30, they fired with accurate precision. The castle's south wall was demolished.

Realizing that it was only a matter of time until the French conquered the castle, the Protestants had no choice but to negotiate a surrender. They were promised by the French that they would be sent to France and would then be set free to go to any other country outside of Scotland. Knox and other Protestants were sent aboard a French galley. As they sailed south, Knox and the others must have wondered if they would ever see Scotland again. For Knox, it was not until twelve years later that he returned to Scotland permanently to assist the Protestant Reformation.

***

In the travel section that follows, we will take you to the seaside town of St Andrews to explore the richness of Scotland's Reformation history. We will visit St Leonard's College, where Knox studied; the Holy Trinity Church, where Knox preached his first sermon; the ruins of the cathedral; the castle, where Knox and the Protestants were besieged; and the Martyrs' Monument, where the martyrs who died for their Protestant faith are commemorated.

Travel: St Andrews

Located on the beautiful east coast of Fife, St Andrews is a small seaside town with a population of about sixteen thousand. A town now famous for golfing, it was Scotland's ecclesiastical capital before the Reformation. Its cathedral was the seat of the archbishop, and its castle was the archbishop's primary residence. Every year, thousands of pilgrims flocked into the town to see the relics of St Andrew. Today, its historic town still retains the medieval street plan where the three main streets—North Street, Market Street, and South Street—converge at the cathedral. The town's significance in Scotland's Reformation makes it a gem to visit.

St Andrews from St Salvator's Tower
© Jamesmcmahon0 / CC BY-SA 1.0.

In the Footsteps of John Knox

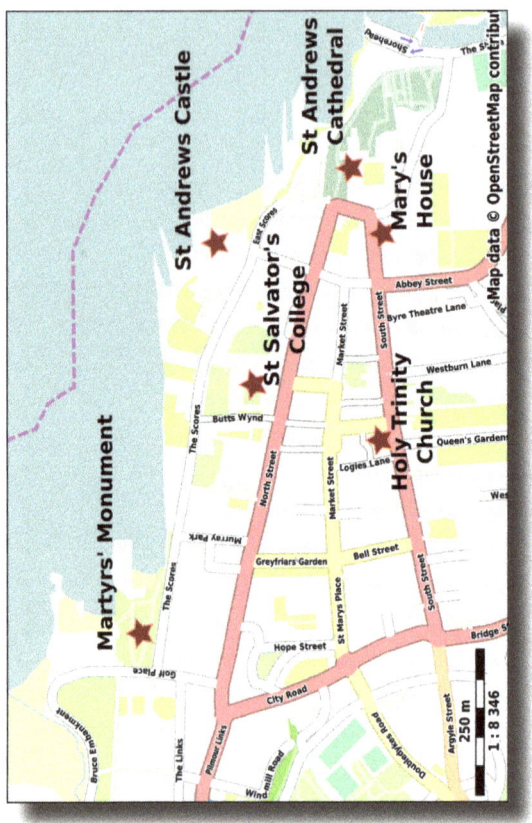

Map of St Andrews

St Andrews University

St Andrews University is the oldest university in Scotland and the third-oldest university in the English-speaking world. Prior to the establishment of St Andrews, Scottish students who wished to pursue higher education had to go abroad to England or continental Europe. It was not until 1410 that a group of Scots initiated a school of higher studies. In those days, only the pope could confer a university's recognition and status. The town of St Andrews was chosen, as it was the ecclesiastical center of Scotland, and the university's status was granted by Pope Benedict XIII in 1413. During the course of the university's first 150 years, it expanded to include St Salvator's College (1450), St Leonard's College (1511), and St Mary's College (1538).

St Salvator's College

St Salvator's College was founded by James Kennedy, Bishop of St Andrews, in 1450. It is also known as "the Old College." The intention of the college was to serve missionary and educational functions. The college was Bishop Kennedy's attempt to improve the theological education of the Scottish clergy. From its establishment, the college saw itself as part of the community. This is apparent in the main entrance to the college's chapel, which faces out onto the streets and not into the college courtyard, a symbol that the church is for the world.

Courtyard of United College, St Andrews University
© Jared and Corin / CC BY-SA 2.0.

Knox spent several years studying at St Salvator's College. Although there are virtually no written records of his years at St Salvator's, Knox must have heard of the burning of Protestant professor Patrick Hamilton, and learned the criticisms of the church hierarchy, from Mair. Like many other students, he likely spent many hours praying and meditating in the college's chapel.

Courtyard of St Salvator's College
© Remi Mathis / CC BY-SA 3.0.

During the long siege of St Andrews Castle (1546–1547), it was here on the tower of St Salvator's that the French set up their cannons to bombard the south castle wall, forcing the Protestants to surrender.

In the Footsteps of John Knox

Patrick Hamilton's Martyrdom

At the front of the red clock tower is the entrance to the college; pink cobbles set into the road form the initials PH. This marks the spot where the young scholar Hamilton was burned at the stake in 1528. See more on the Martyrs' Monument.

Cobblestones create the initials of Patrick Hamilton (PH) on the ground
© Remi Mathis / CC BY-SA 3.0.

St Salvator's Chapel

St Salvator's Chapel is one of the most beautiful medieval churches in the town, exemplifying Gothic architecture. However, many of the medieval decorations—statues, icons, stained glass, and paintings—were removed during the time of the Reformation. It was not until the nineteenth century that stained glass was gradually added back. A few other architectural embellishments were also added, including the Chalmers Memorial to those students who lost their lives in World War I.

St Salvator's Chapel
© Andy Hawkins / CC BY-SA 2.0.

Inside the chapel is also a pulpit supposedly used by Knox. Tradition says that the pulpit came from Holy Trinity Church, where Knox used it while he preached. In reality, the pulpit likely dates from the early seventeenth century instead of from Knox's time.

Interior of the chapel
© Sven Marnach / CC BY-SA 3.0.

Museum of St Andrews University

The museum includes well-documented medieval artifacts, scientific equipment, and an exhibit on the Scottish Reformation. Notable artifacts include the pulpit from which Knox actually preached in Holy Trinity Church in 1559, which incited the destruction of the cathedral.

Deans Court

Located directly across from the ruins of St Andrews Cathedral is the spot where former priest Walter Milne was burned at the stake in 1558 for his opposition to celibacy in the clergy. One year later, when the Reformation campaign came to St Andrews, crowds brought the icons and wooden statues from the church and burned them at the same spot. For more on Walter Milne, see Martyrs' Monument.

The entrance to Deans Court
© Irlmex / CC BY-SA 3.0.

St Andrews Castle

Now a ruin, St Andrews Castle was the residence of the archbishop before the Scottish Reformation. The castle gradually fell into ruin after the Reformation.

Ruins of St Andrews Castle
© Ian Nab82ba / CC BY-SA 3.0.

George Wishart, the Protestant reformer whom Knox admired greatly, was burned at the stake by the order of Archbishop Beaton at the entrance of the castle in 1546. The spot where he died is marked with the initials "GW." It was also in this castle that Knox was called to be a preacher after the Protestants captured the castle.

Initials of George Wishart, at the location where he was burned at the stake
© Kim Traynor / CC BY-SA 2.0.

St Andrews Cathedral

Once the largest church in Scotland, St Andrews Cathedral was the ecclesiastical center of Scotland before the Reformation. Like St Andrews Castle, the cathedral gradually became a ruin. Today, the site features the remains of the cathedral and cloister, a graveyard, and a small exhibit and climbable tower. From the remains of the cathedral, one can see the architectural changes over the 150 years during which the cathedral was built, from Romanesque windows to Gothic arches. Today, the tower of St Rule's offers a spectacular view of the town.

The remaining of the cathedral
© KPapageorgiou / CC BY-SA 4.0.

After Wishart was arrested in January 1546, he was brought to St Andrews. It was here on March 1, 1546, that he was tried by the church court presided over by Archbishop Beaton. He was eventually burned at the stake outside St Andrews Castle. Later, when Scotland's Protestant movement was in a heated stage in 1559, decorations including images and altars were removed from inside the cathedral. As Protestantism gained a foothold after 1560, the building was gradually abandoned. Slowly, the cathedral became a ruin as people took away stones for building materials. It was not until the nineteenth century that attempts were made to preserve what remained of the cathedral.

The surrounding graveyard dates from the post-Reformation era. In it are buried many notable people, including Scotland's famous seventeenth-century theologian Samuel Rutherford (1600–1661). A Presbyterian minister and professor at the divinity school in St Andrews, he was one of the Scottish commissioners to the Westminster Assembly, which formulated the Westminster Confession of Faith. His political writing, *The Law and the Prince*, which advocated limited government and constitutionalism, as well as his theory regarding church and state, had a profound impact on the development of democracy in the Western world.

The Martyrs' Monument

The Martyrs' Monument was erected in 1842 to commemorate four Protestant martyrs from the sixteenth century: Patrick Hamilton, Henry Forrest, George Wishart, and Walter Milne. These martyrs paved the way for the Scottish Reformation.

The Martyrs' Monument
© Kim Traynor / CC BY-SA 3.0.

Patrick Hamilton (c.1504–1528)

Hamilton, a distinctive young professor at St Andrews University, encountered Protestant thought while studying at Paris and Louvain. He promoted Martin Luther's thought after returning to Scotland. Soon, he was arrested by the Roman Catholic authority and burned at the stake on February 29, 1528. Patrick Hamilton's initials (PH) can be found in the cobblestones on North Street (in front of the entrance to St Salvator's College), the spot where he was burned.

Henry Forrest (c.?–1533)

Henry Forrest was originally a Benedictine monk and priest. When the Catholic authority discovered that he was reading the New Testament in English, they suspended his role in the church. He also spoke against the execution of Patrick Hamilton. He was arrested and executed in 1533 outside the north end of the Cathedral, the highest point in St Andrews.

George Wishart (c. 1513–1546)

Executed at the age of thirty-three at the entrance of St Andrews Castle, Wishart had a profound influence on Knox. Like Hamilton, he was educated in continental Europe. He was greatly influenced by the thoughts of Luther and John Calvin. When he returned to Scotland, he preached across the country to promote church reform. He was arrested in 1546 and sent to St Andrews Castle, then burned at the stake on Easter of 1546 at the castle's entrance.

Walter Milne (c.?–1558)

Milne was executed outside Deans Court in 1558. He was a Catholic priest but left the priesthood to be married. He was burned at the stake because he believed that priests should be allowed the freedom to marry.

Queen Mary's House

This was the residence where Mary, Queen of Scots, stayed when she visited St Andrews. She liked the place so much that she eventually acquired the house. When she was in St Andrews, she would "roam incognito through the streets with her maids of honour, her former childhood playmates known as the 'four Maries.' Her 'Maries' assisted her, and a special 'kitchen' was created in their apartments so that they could play at cooking and housekeeping."[10]

Queen Mary's House
© Kilnburn / Wikimedia Commons.

---

10 John A. Guy, *My Heart Is My Own: The Life of Mary Queen of Scots* (London: Fourth Estate, 2009).

Here in this house, Mary made key decisions that would alter the course of Scottish history. In 1565, she sat in her house by the Abbey to discuss whom she should marry. It was then that she set her sights upon Lord Darnley. This decision eventually led to her abdication.

Holy Trinity Church

This was the church where John Knox preached his first sermon during the siege of St Andrews Castle in 1547. When he was forced to serve as a slave on the French galley, lying very sick, he said that he would come back here to preach one day. Twelve years later, when the wave of Reformation swept across Scotland, he returned to St Andrews and fulfilled his own words. Like many churches that have stood since the sixteenth century, this church has been renovated.

The tower of Holy Trinity Church
© Kilnburn / CC BY-SA 2.0.

Chapter 3: Exile in England (1547–1554)

Slave on a French Galley

In August 1547, Knox and other Protestant prisoners were deported from St Andrews Castle to France by sea. Their galley arrived at the French coast near the River Seine. From there, the galley went upriver and stopped at the town of Rouen. The prisoners were hoping that they would be released and allowed to settle in other Protestant states, as they had been promised at the time of their surrender at St Andrews Castle. Instead, the ordinary Scots on the galley were condemned to slavery while the nobles were imprisoned within French castles.

Knox and other Scots commoners were given galley slaves' brown woolen robes to wear, and they were chained by leg irons to their rowing bench. The conditions were harsh. It took six men to ply the oars. Knox and other slaves worked in shifts. If they showed signs of fatigue, they would be punished. They were only given water to drink and ship's biscuits to eat, with vegetable soup three times a week. During the winter months when sea conditions were rough, they had to continue to work repairing the sails.

The Scots were also expected to attend Mass. However, they found ways to humiliate the French Catholic practices. When the French on board sang "Salve Regina," the anthem of the Blessed Virgin Mary, the Scots pulled their caps and hoods down over their ears to block the sound. On another occasion, when a painting of the Virgin Mary was passed around the decks so that everyone could kiss it, Knox refused to take it and said, "Such an idol is accursed; and, therefore I will not touch it."[11] The officer ordered him to take it and thrust it to his face, placing the image in his hand. After the image had been placed in his

---

11 John Knox, *The History of the Reformation of Religion in Scotland* (Glasgow: Blackie, Fullarton, & Co., 1831), 78.

hand, he looked at it and cast it into the river, saying, "Let our Lady now save herself; she is light enough; let her learn to swim."[12] Knox did not record whether they were punished for such behaviors or not. Their determination forced the officer to stop forcing Catholic practices onto them.

While a slave in the French galley, Knox continued his pastoral role to his fellow Scots. He comforted those who were afraid and weak in spirit. When his friend James Balfour of Pittendreich was troubled, he turned to Knox for encouragement. Knox often replied and said that "God would deliver them from that bondage, to his glory, even in this life."[13]

The following summer, while on a galley trip to Scotland, Knox became very ill. People thought he was dying. As the galley lay between Dundee and St Andrews, his friend Balfour raised him so that he could see the shore of St Andrews. Balfour asked if he could recognize where he was. Even though Knox was so ill, he raised himself up and gazed toward the tower of the cathedral, the Holy Trinity Church, and St Andrews Cathedral, and replied, "Yes, I know it well; for I see the steeple of that place, where God first opened my mouth in public to his glory, and I am fully persuaded, how weak that ever I now appear, that I shall not depart this life, till that my tongue shall glorify his godly name in the same place."[14]

That same autumn, the galley returned to Rouen in France. As winter arrived, sailing activities on the sea were stopped. Knox was able to spend time reading theological treatises, and he used the winter to correspond with Scottish noble prisoners who were imprisoned in French castles. He also used the time to instruct and strengthen the faith of other Protestant prisoners.

As the weather turned warmer and trees began to leaf out in the spring, the English government held a diplomatic negotiation with France. Knox was included in a prisoner exchange and released. Nineteen months as a slave had a lasting impact; for the rest of Knox's life, he frequently experienced severe headaches and digestive problems.[15] The experience also reinforced what Wishart had taught him: to sepa-

---

12 Ibid.
13 Ibid.
14 Ibid.
15 Knox, *The Works of John Knox*, III:351, 355.

rate the world into "us" and "them." He increasingly polarized everything into two opposite sides.[16]

England: Berwick-upon-Tweed and Newcastle

Freed in the spring of 1549, Knox quickly traveled to London, England. At the time, England was under the reign of King Henry VIII's son, the ten-year-old Edward VI. Knox was already a well-known figure, and he was received warmly in London. The Lord Protector Somerset and the Privy Council invited him to go to the border town Berwick-upon-Tweed to serve as an army chaplain. Berwick-upon-Tweed was close to Scotland and had changed hands several times between the two countries in previous centuries. It was a heavily fortified, strategic town controlled at that time by the English.

Knox preached weekly at St Mary's, the town's parish church. Many Scots would slip over the border and come to listen to him preach. His congregation would consist of Scots, soldiers of the garrisons, citizens, and other middle- and upper-class people from the surrounding area. His fervor, fluency, sardonic humor, and down-to-earth language attracted people from different classes. His experience as a galley slave must have also earned the respect of the soldiers.

As England's Protestantism was still in its infancy, there were still clergy and bishops who supported the Roman Catholic view of the Lord's Supper: that the bread and the wine actually became the body and blood of Christ in the enactment of the Sacrament. Knox totally opposed that view. Therefore, he was summoned by the bishop and the Council of North to explain his viewpoint. His arguments, which were later published as *A Vindication of the Doctrine that the Sacrifice of the Mass is Idolatry*, silenced the council. He was let go.

The peace between England and Scotland toward the end of 1551 meant that England's military establishment could return to its main base, from Berwick-upon-Tweed back to Newcastle. From 1551, Knox was preaching and living in Newcastle. He preached at the Church of St Nicholas regularly. In fact, he was quite busy preaching. In his own account of what happened around Christmas of 1551, he complained that he was still preaching daily even when he was unwell.[17] While he was busily involved in pastoral ministry in Newcastle, he still managed to find the time to visit the church at Berwick-upon-Tweed frequently.

---

16 Dawson, *John Knox*, 53.
17 Ibid., 62.

In Knox's private life, he was betrothed toward the end of 1552. The bride was Marjorie Bowes, the daughter of Knox's close friend Elizabeth Bowes. Elizabeth and her daughter Marjorie had converted to Protestantism from Roman Catholicism, and Elizabeth often wrote to Knox seeking spiritual advice. It was she who suggested this marriage between Knox and her daughter. In today's view, it may sound unusual for a son-in-law and mother-in-law to have such a close relationship. Still, in a sixteenth-century context, it was not unusual for a married woman to seek advice from her clergy.[18]

In the meantime, the political power of England changed hands from Lord Protector Somerset to John Dudley, Duke of Northumberland. The duke, on his tour to inspect the fortifications, took Knox with him as his chaplain. Impressed by Knox's preaching, the duke asked Knox to go south with him. Knox might have felt that his ministry in Newcastle and Berwick-upon-Tweed was not yet over; nevertheless, he left his betrothed wife in the north and traveled with the duke south to King Edward's court.

At King Edward VI's Court

In September of 1552, Knox arrived at King Edward VI's court. At that time, the second revised version of *The Book of Common Prayer*, intended to be used in the Church of England, had just been approved by Parliament and was being printed already. While Knox welcomed the reform aspects of the second edition, he felt there were still Roman Catholic practices present. Specifically, he did not agree with the instruction of kneeling to receive Communion, which he thought was an idolatrous, Roman Catholic practice. That September, Knox preached before King Edward VI and his court at Windsor Castle. In his sermon, he spoke strongly against the posture of kneeling during Communion. As a result of his preaching, a compromise was reached. As *The Book of Common Prayer* was already being printed, a special explanation was inserted. It was called "the Black Rubric," as it was not printed in red ink, but black, due to the shortness of time to publication.

Knox was frustrated by the compromise. Having only served in the parish ministry near the border up north, he did not understand the mindset of the ecclesiastical polity in England. For the Edwardian Church, a compromise was at times necessary to unite the entire nation.

---

18 For a detail discussion on Knox's relationship with Elizabeth Bowes, see Ibid., 65-70.

Knox was soon offered the office of bishop of the diocese of Rochester. He surprised everybody by declining, although he was not against churches having bishops. In this case, he felt that the bishopric would restrict him from preaching. He was then offered the position of minister at All Hallows Church in London. Again, he surprised everyone by refusing this position. Even though Knox always considered his role to be that of a pastor, he might have, at this time, taken the prophetic role more seriously. Instead of simply preaching and focusing on the pastoral ministry in one parish, he preferred the role of roving preacher.[19]

On July 7, 1553, while Knox was on a preaching mission out of London to Buckinghamshire, King Edward VI died. Edward VI named his Protestant cousin, Lady Jane Grey, to the throne. However, her reign only lasted a few days. On July 19, she was replaced by Edward's Roman Catholic half-sister, Mary Tudor. Many prominent Protestants were arrested in London. Knox was glad to be out of London and safe from arrest.

In the fall of 1553, while deciding whether or not to leave England, he traveled to England's northeast to see his betrothed wife Marjorie, as he feared that he might never be able to see her again. Urged by his friends, he departed England that winter. He was in exile again, not sure where God would lead him.

***

In the travel section that follows, we will visit England's northeastern frontier, the once heavily fortified town of Berwick-upon-Tweed, and the industrial city of Newcastle-upon-Tyne.

---

19 Ibid., 78.

Travel: England

BERWICK-UPON-TWEED

Berwick-upon-Tweed is the northernmost town in England, about four kilometers south of the border with Scotland. During the two centuries before 1482, the town switched hands between England and Scotland more than fourteen times. It has remained in English hands since 1482. Knox must have felt at home there, as there were many Scottish descendants who lived there. There were also many Scottish merchants who would bring news from Scotland.

Street view of Berwick-upon-Tweed
© Robertallen1992 / CC BY-SA 3.0.

When Knox arrived here in the spring of 1549, he discovered that the town was overcrowded with military guards, as it was England's most northerly frontier and served as the post for England's military campaign against Scotland. The medieval walls that Knox encountered as he entered the city were twenty-two feet high. There were also nineteen towers, five arched gates, and a system of ditches. This fortification that Knox encountered was built in the early fourteenth century under Edward I. In 1560, a new set of fortifications was constructed, which destroyed much of the medieval wall structure. As the walls were built during the reign of Elizabeth I, they were known as the Elizabethan walls.

Part of the Elizabethan walls
© Nilfanion / CC BY-SA 3.0.

Outside the wall, close to the banks of the Tweed, was Berwick Castle. The castle today has disintegrated into ruins. In Knox's time, the castle had a large garrison but was without any barracks. It was a vital stronghold, as it is located along the disputed border between England and Scotland. However, the building structure began a steady decline soon afterward. A significant percentage of the stones were taken to build the town's parish church in England's Commonwealth era. Today, only the ruins of the castle still remain.

In the Footsteps of John Knox

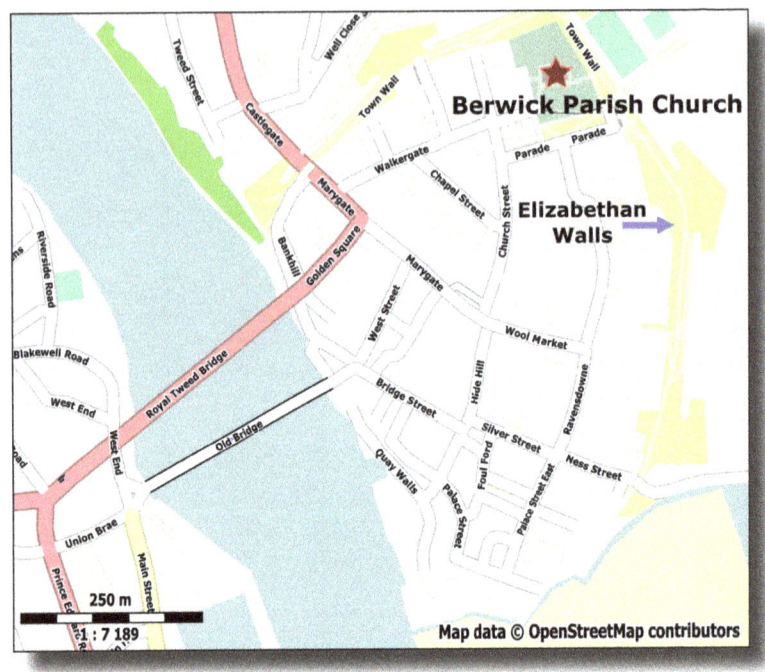

Map of Berwick-upon-Tweed

St Mary's Parish (Berwick Parish Church)

St Mary's, the parish church where Knox served as a minister, was in the center of Berwick. However, the original church building (dating back to medieval times) no longer existed. In 1652, during the Commonwealth of England, a new church building was erected a few yards north of the original building. The building materials included many of the stones from nearby Berwick castle. After the completion of the new building, the original building was demolished. The church today houses what is thought to be the pulpit built for Knox during his ministry in Berwick-upon-Tweed. In the nineteenth century, stained-glass windows and a chancel were installed in the building.

Knox had great success in his ministry at Berwick. His preaching drew large crowds. Scots slipped across the city wall and came to hear him preach every week. It was here that he first preached consistently. His leadership brought order to the chaotic community in Berwick.[20]

---

20 Marshall, *John Knox*, chap. 3.

Berwick Parish Church
© James@hopgrove / CC BY-SA 2.0.

NEWCASTLE

Located in northeast England, sixty miles south of Berwick-upon-Tweed, the city of Newcastle acted as an important hub for the region. Its origin can be dated back to Roman settlement. The city was also located at the end of the Hadrian's Wall, a defensive fortification built by the Romans, stretching from the Irish Sea to the banks of River Tyne. In the medieval period leading to the time of Reformation, the city played a major role in the wars between England and Scotland. It was successfully defended against Scottish invasion several times in the fourteenth century. In the sixteenth century, the city was already well-known for its port and shipping industry.

A view of the city
© JimmyGuano / CC BY-SA 4.0.

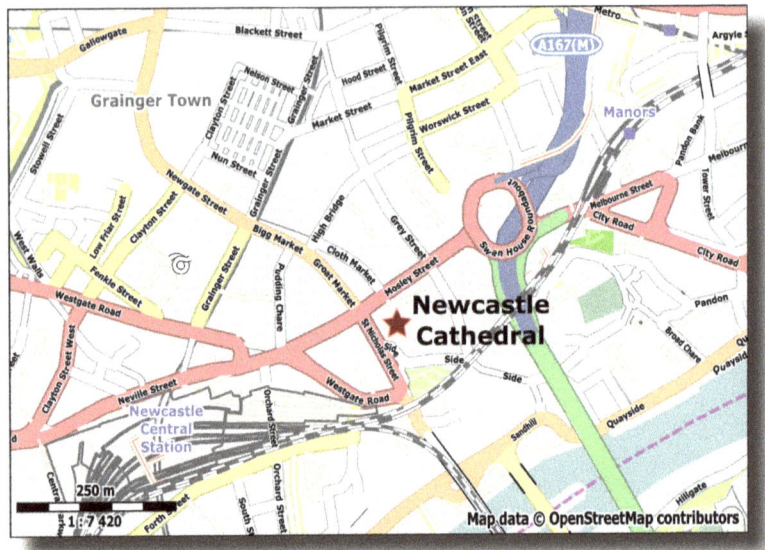

Map of Newcastle

St Nicholas Cathedral (Newcastle Cathedral)

The current building of St Nicholas Cathedral was completed in the fourteenth century. Its magnificent Gothic building with a lantern tower dominates the skyline of Newcastle. During the English Civil War in 1640, the interior of the cathedral was severely damaged by the Scots. Again in 1646, when the city was besieged by Scots for nine weeks, the Scots threatened to destroy the lantern tower by bombardment. However, they were dissuaded when the mayor of the city placed Scottish prisoners in the tower.

After Knox moved to Newcastle, he served as the preacher of St Nicholas Cathedral from 1551 to 1553. By Knox's own account, he was busy serving in the church even during the weekdays. He was able to develop and confirm his pastoral identity as a pastor, preacher, and prophet. The ministry in Newcastle as well as that of Berwick brought him a great sense of fulfilment.[21] There were also moments in which he admitted that he felt the spiritual temptation of pride.[22]

---

21 Dawson, *John Knox*, 68-69.
22 Knox, *The Works of John Knox*, III:317.

St Nicholas Cathedral (Newcastle Cathedral)
© JimmyGuano / CC BY-SA 4.0.

OTHER PLACES IN ENGLAND

Whitehall Palace

Whitehall Palace was the primary residence of English monarchy for much of the sixteenth and seventeenth centuries. It was once the largest palace in Europe, with more than 1,500 rooms.

It was in Whitehall Palace that Knox delivered the Lenten sermons in the Chapel Royal before the king and his court in April of 1553. This series of sermons caused Knox great trouble. In one of the sermons, he preached on the theme of corruption, in which leaders are often ill-served by their advisers. In the sermon, he pointed out that King David in the Old Testament was ill-served by his advisers—and that even Jesus had Judas among his disciples.[23] There is no doubt that this

---

23 Peter Lorimer, *John Knox and the Church of England* (London: Henry S. King, 1875), 171–75.

caused great uneasiness among the courtiers to whom he preached. As a result of this sermon, he was summoned before the Privy Council on April 14, 1553.

Much of the palace, including the Chapel Royal where Knox preached his Lenten sermons to King Edward VI's court, was destroyed by a great fire in 1698. The only major building remaining today is the banquet hall.

Windsor Castle

Located in the English county of Berkshire, Windsor Castle was built in the eleventh century. It has been used by all England's monarchy as a residence since the time of Henry I, making it the longest-occupied palace in Europe. When the Duke of Northumberland traveled south, he took Knox with him as his chaplain. It was here in Windsor Castle where Knox was invited to preach before the young King Edward VI at the end of September of 1552. In the sermon, he preached against the kneeling practice of receiving Communion in *The Book of Common Prayer*, which eventually led to the insertion of an explanation page in the book.

Windsor Castle
© Petr.noha / CC BY-SA 3.0.

Chapter 4: Frankfurt

Knox left England and arrived at the French port of Dieppe in January of 1554. His brother William had trading links with Scottish merchants in the town, and this was likely the reason he chose Dieppe as his initial destination. He stayed in this French port for several weeks, hoping to receive any news from Marjorie and her mother Elizabeth. While waiting at the port, he was able to complete his exposition of Psalm 6 and several tracts. Psalm 6, a Psalm of David in the midst of trouble pleading to the Lord for help, was parallel to Knox's own situation. He had been enslaved in a French galley, and the Lord delivered him. Now, he had to flee England and see many Protestants being persecuted; he could not help but cry to the Lord, echoing David, "Have mercy on me, Lord, for I am faint; heal me, Lord, for my bones are in agony. My soul is in deep anguish. How long, Lord, how long? Turn, Lord, and deliver me; save me because of your unfailing love...I am worn out from my groaning" (Psalm 6, NIV).

Seeking Advice

By early 1554, Knox was deeply troubled by the situation in England. In addition to those being persecuted, many people simply started to attend Mass again. In his letters, Knox urged Protestants to keep their faith and not attend Roman Catholic worship. His troubled heart comes through clearly in a letter sent to England, which he ends with, "From a sore troubled heart upon my departure from Dieppe, whither God knoweth."[24]

Having witnessed a shift of religious policies after the succession of Catholic queen Mary Tudor following the death of the teenage king, and the fear of foreign intervention after the marriage proposal between the queen and the Catholic king, Philip of Spain, Knox was

---

24 Knox, *The Works of John Knox*, III:184ff.

troubled by four specific questions:

- What was the legitimacy of the male minor who came to the throne?
- What was the legitimacy of the female ruler, and could the reigning queen transfer regal authority to her husband?
- What must people do if the ruler enforces idolatry (e.g. Roman Catholic practices)?
- What was the legitimacy of active resistance by Protestant nobles against their Roman Catholic rulers?

In search of direction, Knox decided to travel 800 miles south to Switzerland. His first stop was in the city of Geneva, where the French Protestant theologian John Calvin resided. A native of France, Calvin was the Protestant leader in the city of Geneva. Calvin achieved widespread fame in the Christian world with the publication of the first edition of *The Institutes of Christian Religion* in 1536, and Knox thought to seek Calvin's advice on his troubles.

In 1554, Calvin was in the midst of challenging situations, such as the trial of Servetus; his opponents, the Libertines, were also giving him a difficult time. As Knox showed up unexpectedly, Calvin was busy and could only briefly respond to his questions. Calvin basically expressed to him that the subjects should obey their ruler, regardless of anything else. Knowing that Knox was not satisfied, on March 9 Calvin sent Knox to see other reformers in Switzerland with letters of recommendation.

Knox traveled along Lake Geneva to Lausanne to meet with Theodore Beza and Pierre Viret. His final destination was Zurich, where he met Zwingli's successor, Heinrich Bullinger. The only evidence of the trip that survived was Bullinger's set of responses to Knox's questions. Bullinger went further than Calvin, saying that it was not necessary for subjects to obey a ruler who enforced idolatry. However, like Calvin, Bullinger did not want to endorse any forms of active resistance. Neither encouraged nor discouraged, Knox ended his travel and returned to the port of Dieppe.

Frankfurt

In the summer of 1554, Knox was still troubled and depressed. He did not know where to go. In the midst of this uncertainty, he traveled south to Geneva again. He thought to use this interlude to pursue more theological studies under Calvin. A few months into his studies, he received a letter of invitation from a group of English exiles in Frankfurt at the beginning of October of 1554; they invited him to be their pastor.

Located on the banks of the River Main, Frankfurt was a Protestant city within the Holy Roman Empire. The city had adopted Lutheranism, a form of Protestantism, in 1533. Before the English exiles arrived, the city had already provided shelter to a congregation of French Protestants. When Knox received the news, depressed and troubled, he only wanted to retreat back to his studies. It was Calvin who pushed him to accept the offer. Calvin encouraged Knox to take up this challenge, saying that those who lead church and society into transformation were those who had extensive practical experience.[25]

In November 1554, Knox set out on the lengthy journey from Geneva to Frankfurt. He likely traveled around Lake Geneva and went north along the River Rhine.

By the time Knox arrived at Frankfurt, it was the third week of November. He found himself in the midst of a crisis over the issue of liturgy used in *The Book of Common Prayer*. Since the English exiles shared the building of the Church of the White Ladies with the French refugee community, the city authority granted the English exiles permission to use the church building on the condition that the English use a form of service similar to that of the French Calvinists. It was agreed by everyone that some forms of alteration to *The Book of Common Prayer* were necessary to remove any direct offense either to the city or to the French community. The question was this: To what extent must *The Book of Common Prayer* be changed? There were those who thought that minimal change was necessary, and there were those who would have liked to seize the chance to amend the 1552 version of the book.

Knox was immediately drawn into this conflict. Due to his previous criticism of *The Book of Common Prayer*, he was seen by those who supported drastic change as their ally. His uncompromising style stirred up even more conflict when he announced to the congregation that he would not be able to administer the Lord's Supper according to *The Book of Common Prayer*. Both sides sought support from the mag-

---

25 Marshall, *John Knox*, chap. 6.

istrates and other leading reformers in continental Europe, including Calvin, Bullinger, and Peter Martyr Vermigli. It was an overwhelming situation for Knox to handle. Less than two months into his ministry, he was already seeking ways to quit.

Toward the end of that year and the beginning of the next year, a committee of five people was established within the congregation to deal with the matter. For a while, it seemed that all matters went smoothly, yet it was only the quiet before a new storm. On March 13, a large group of English exiles led by Richard Cox arrived from Strasbourg, insisting on the usage of *The Book of Common Prayer*. A congregational meeting was held on March 19. While it was obvious that the newcomers wanted to gain admission to the congregation to support the use of *The Book of Common Prayer*, Knox was mistakenly overconfident admitting them. As soon as these newcomers were allowed to vote, Knox's opponents gained enough votes in their favor to dismiss him from his pastoral duty in Frankfurt.

In the midst of these conflicts, he was also reported by his enemies to the city for the charge of treason against Emperor Charles V for having published the work *Faithful Admonition* the previous year. In that work, Knox denounced Queen Mary Tudor and her husband, Philip II of Spain. Emperor Charles V of the Holy Roman Empire happened to be the uncle of Philip II. Although the charge was never established, Knox was already exhausted.

On the evening of March 25, 1555, Knox preached his farewell sermon to about fifty sympathizers in the congregation. He left Frankfurt the next day and set out for Geneva again, after just four months of ministry in Frankfurt.

A Brief Trip Back to Scotland

Wounded and exhausted, Knox came back to Geneva to resume his theological studies. As England was still persecuting Protestants, he was concerned about the safety of Marjorie Bowes. A few months into his studies, he departed Geneva and headed to Scotland. He hoped to travel from Scotland to northeastern England to meet with Marjorie and bring her to Geneva. Knox had also heard from his friends of the promising progress of Protestantism in Scotland. For Knox, it seemed a good time to travel home. He hoped to return back to Geneva by December of 1555.

Knox traveled to the port of Dieppe. With the help of Scottish merchants, he was able to return to Scotland smoothly. He arrived in Edinburgh in late September of 1555. His exile status had made him widely known among Scottish Protestants, and many came to meet him. He was surprised by the progress of the development of Protestantism in Scotland. In a letter written to Elizabeth Bowes, he stated, "If I had not seen it with my own eyes in my own country, I could not have believed it."[26] Despite the success of Protestantism, Knox was also concerned. Now that the regency was in the hand of Mary of Guise, the queen's mother and a devout Catholic, he saw many Protestant nobles still attending Mass at the royal court in order to please her. Knox was horrified. He stressed that they must stop attending Mass.

During his stay in Scotland, his activities were mostly limited to private gatherings. His original plan to come back to Geneva by the end of December of 1555 was extended well into the spring of 1556. His travels took him from Edinburgh to southwest Scotland and many other places. By April, despite remaining low-key, his activities caught the attention of the Roman Catholic authorities. He was summoned to appear on a charge of heresy by Archbishop John Hamilton. The public meeting would take place on May 15, 1556, in Black Friars' Church in Edinburgh. Without showing any fear, Knox decided to attend. The queen regent, Mary of Guise, sensed that this might cause public riots and persuaded Archbishop Hamilton to withdraw the charge.

Knox preached publicly in Edinburgh instead. His powerful preaching inspired those who attended the service. Protestants were convinced that if the queen regent herself heard him preach, she would be converted to Protestantism. With encouragement from the Protestants, he wrote a letter to Mary of Guise to entice her to Protestantism. Initially, he waited hopefully for her response. However, as days went by, his hopes turned to disappointment. There was simply no response. Meanwhile, a letter came from Geneva inviting Knox to be one of the pastors of the English exiles there. Realizing that it could only be a matter of time until Scotland's Catholic authority acted against him again, Knox decided to leave the country once more.

It was around this time that he finally married Marjorie Bowes. There are no details of how this transpired. It was possible that when Knox was in Ayrshire, he returned secretly to Northumberland (north-

---

26 Knox, *The Works of John Knox*, IV:216–17.

east England) to meet with Marjorie and they then traveled back to Scotland again.[27] Marjorie's mother Elizabeth also joined them around this time. We do not know why Elizabeth left her husband, but it is possible that being a devout Protestant, she felt that it would be better to leave the country. The couple likely were married in Edinburgh.

In July 1556, Knox left Scotland and headed to Dieppe to meet Marjorie and Elizabeth, as he had already sent them to Dieppe first. What he thought would be a trip of a few months extended into the summer of the following year. For Knox, the trip was fruitful. He had not only become a married man, but he was also able to establish contact with many important Protestant nobles, including Archibald Campbell; Lord Lorne, heir to the Earl of Argyll; and John Lord Erskine, the later Regent Mar. These three would later become important figures in the effort to overthrow Mary of Guise and eventually establish Scotland as a Protestant nation.

***

In the travel section that follows, we will visit two continental cities: the glamorous port of Dieppe and the German city of Frankfurt, the site of Knox's short-lived ministry. Geneva, the city close to Lake Geneva, which Knox regarded as "the most perfect school in Christ since the time of Apostles," will be introduced after chapter 5.

---

27 Dawson, *John Knox*, 111.

Travel: Dieppe and Frankfurt

DIEPPE, FRANCE

A view of the city of Dieppe
© Georgio / CC BY-SA 3.0.

Dieppe is a port in upper Normandy, well known for the failed Allied forces' landing operation during World War II. It was an important port in the eleventh century, linking William the Conqueror's England with his Normandy territory. In the sixteenth century, it was a busy trading port. Many Scottish merchants also settled here. Knox's brother William likely had trading links with the Scottish community in Dieppe.

Knox chose this port as his main hub to travel back and forth across the English Channel because of the convenience and the presence of its Scottish community. Unsure where to go after Mary Tudor came to the throne in England, Knox arrived here on January 20, 1554 before discerning his next stop. He also used this port as his hub to travel to Scotland in 1556, 1557, and 1559.

At this port, Knox started or completed many of his important writings. It was here in early 1554, after he fled from England, that he completed the exposition of Psalm 6 and several tracts that he had been composing since the previous year. In 1557, upon receiving an invitation from the nobles of Scotland indicating that they were prepared to risk their lives to introduce changes in Scotland in favor of the Protestant faith, Knox traveled here only to receive the news that the nobility had changed their minds. While he was waiting in Dieppe, he composed *The First Blast of the Trumpet*, *The Appellation to the Nobility and Estates*, and *A Letter Addressed to the Commonalty of Scotland*.

FRANKFURT, GERMANY

Situated on the banks of the River Main, Frankfurt was an important European trading and communication hub. The invention of the printing press made the city famous for publishing and the book trade in the sixteenth century. Book fairs were held every Easter and Michaelmas. After Mary Tudor came to the throne, Frankfurt became one of the main cities in continental Europe where English exiles settled. When considering which city he would choose, English exile John Scory listed Frankfurt's many advantages: "cheap food, benevolent magistrates, humane people, fair houses and wholesome air...[and] the beer was good."[28] Today, much of the old town reveals destruction from World War II. Although efforts to rebuild began immediately after the war, the town now has a completely different feel from Knox's time.

---

28 Quoted in Ibid., 91.

The Old Town today
© Mylius / CC BY-SA 3.0.

The Church of White Ladies (*Weißfrauenkirche*)

The Church of White Ladies was originally built in the thirteenth century as part of a monastery. After the Reformation, the church was converted to Protestant use. The city council permitted French Huguenots to worship here, and after the English exiles arrived, they were assigned by the city to use the same space. It was here that Knox ministered as the pastor of the English exiles from the end of 1554 until March of 1555. Overwhelmed by the congregation's divided opinion on the use of liturgy, he left in late March of 1555.

Unfortunately, none of the church structure survived World War II. After the war, the city offered the congregation a different location to rebuild its church.

Chapter 5: The Most Perfect School of Christ

For Knox, the experience of exile was "to be in such a straight as those that from realm to realm and city to city seek rest as pilgrims and yet shall find none."[29] He found shelter in England and treated the place as his adopted home but was forced to leave when Mary Tudor came to the throne. The call to be minister at the Frankfurt English congregation was short-lived due to the dispute over liturgy. Although exile was not pleasant, one place that he would always treasure was Geneva. He enjoyed it so much that in a letter to a friend, he wrote that it was the "most perfect school of Christ that ever was on earth since the days of the Apostles."[30] Geneva appealed to Knox because of "the public maintenance of the laws of God and the consequent reformation of behaviour"[31] that he had so far not experienced in other places.

After the short trip back to Scotland, Knox crossed to Dieppe in mid-July to meet Marjorie and his mother-in-law, who had arrived here earlier. A few weeks later, they traveled together to Geneva, where Knox was called to be the minister of the exiled English congregation. In September 1556, Knox and the whole family were admitted as members of the English congregation in Geneva.

Unlike the English congregation in Frankfurt, the English exiles in Geneva were very supportive of Knox's ministry. They allowed him to respond to various calls from Scotland, and when Knox had to be away, he did not have to worry about the ministry of the congregation. His team ministry with Christopher Goodman also proved successful, as they shared similar visions. Knox's new wife, Marjorie, assisted him greatly in his ministry. She acted as his secretary and assisted him with his writings. She was loved and accepted by the congregation. Calvin

---

29 Knox, *The Works of John Knox*, IV:219.
30 Ibid., IV:240.
31 Dawson, *John Knox*, 151.

even described her as "the most delightful of wives."[32] In Geneva she bore Knox two sons: Nathaniel, on May 23, 1557, and Eleazer on November 29, 1558.

The Geneva Bible

While in Geneva, Knox and the English congregation undertook the important project of translating the Bible into English. It was not the first English translation, but it was the first English Bible to have verse numbers. Other key features of this Bible were interpretations included in the marginal notes section, woodcut illustrations, and maps. It was virtually the first English Study Bible. Key scholars involved included Knox, William Whittingham, Calvin, Myles Cloverdale, John Fox, and others. The features of this Bible, and the fact that it was translated by internationally known scholars, made the Geneva Bible widely popular in the English world until the introduction of the King James Bible in the early seventeenth century.

A Trip to Scotland Halted at Dieppe

Shortly after his son Nathaniel was born, Knox received a letter inviting him back to Scotland. It was written by Protestant nobles Lord Lorne, the Earl of Glencair, Lord James Stewart, and Lord Erskine, whom Knox had met on his Scottish trip the previous year. In the letter, the nobles indicated that they would be "ready to jeopard lives and goods in the forward setting of the glory of God."[33] The invitation was difficult for Knox to evaluate. On one hand, he felt that he was called to ministry by the English exiles. On the other hand, he felt the need to lead the Reformation in Scotland. It was difficult to discern where God was calling him. Therefore, he consulted the flocks of his congregation and the Genevan pastors, including Calvin. The advice was unambiguous: "That he could not refuse that vocation [to return to Scotland] unless he would declare himself rebellious unto his God, and unmerciful to his country."[34]

Knox knew that even though he had the Protestant nobles' support, the trip back to Scotland would be risky and dangerous. Proper planning and strategy were necessary. It took him a few more months before he finally set out. While preparing for the trip, he made use of the time to be with his family. In September 1557, he left Geneva.

---

32 Knox, *The Works of John Knox*, IV:124–5.
33 Ibid., IV:256.
34 Ibid., I:133.

When he arrived at Dieppe on October 24, 1557, he received a letter from the Protestant nobles that instructed him to stay and wait in Dieppe. They no longer thought that it was the right time, and they themselves wavered. Knox was angry and confused, as it had taken him a great effort to arrange the trip and to travel from Geneva. He was even prepared to risk his life for the cause of Reformation in Scotland.

Three days later, on October 27, he wrote to the Protestant nobles: "I partly was confounded, and partly was pierced with anguish and sorrow."[35] He reminded the nobles that they were the princes of the people and were not elevated by their noble status at birth, "by reason of your office and duty, which is to vindicate and deliver your subjects and brethren from all violence and oppression, to the uttermost of your power."[36]

If he were to return to Geneva then, it would look very bad for the Protestant movement in Scotland, and for Knox himself. In addition, the war between France and England continued on the continent, making it difficult to return to Geneva. Therefore, Knox decided to stay in Dieppe and await further news. By February of 1558, there was still no positive word from Scotland. By this time, the continental war zone had shifted north, providing a safer route for Knox to travel back to Geneva. He packed his belongings and returned.

Back in Geneva, he returned to pastoral ministry to the English congregation. Aside from pastoral tasks, he put considerable attention into writings intended to respond to the situations in England and Scotland. Three notable writings were published: *The First Blast of the Trumpet*, *The Appellation to the Nobility*, and *The Letter to the Commonalty*.

The First Blast of the Trumpet

For contemporary readers, the full title of the book *The First Blast of the Trumpet against the Monstrous Regiment of Women* can be misleading. However, in the sixteenth century, "regiment" meant rule, and "monstrous" meant unnatural. Knox was attacking the unnatural rule of women. More specifically, he was attacking Queen Mary Tudor of England because she was persecuting Protestants. The first main point in this work was Knox's belief that the rule of women was contrary to natural and divine law. He allowed some exceptions, but the then-current queen of England, Mary Tudor, was not one of them, since she fol-

---

35 Knox, *The History of the Reformation of Religion in Scotland*, 92.
36 Ibid., 93.

lowed Catholic practices and persecuted Protestants. The second point that Knox emphasized was that if a monarchy were idolatrous, active resistance was necessary to remove it. This second point was radical in his time. Even Calvin and Bullinger only supported passive resistance.

Knox published *The First Blast* in the context of Catholic Queen Mary Tudor's persecution in England. However, the timing was not right. The book went to publication only a few months before the death of Mary Tudor. Mary's Protestant half-sister, Elizabeth, succeeded her and was not amused by Knox's view on female rulers or with his resistance theory. Calvin and many of the English exiles in Geneva also spoke or wrote against *The First Blast*.

The Appellation to the Nobility and *The Letter to the Commonalty*

After *The First Blast* was completed, Knox turned his attention to the situation in Scotland. He wrote two public letters to Scotland: *The Appellation to the Nobility* and *The Letter to the Commonalty*. Having experienced the nobles' indecision at Dieppe, in *The Appellation to the Nobility* he upbraided the nobility for their indecision and at the same time reminded them of their "office and duty" to "vindicate and deliver [their] subjects from all violence and oppression to the uttermost of [their] power."[37] Having completed this letter, Knox felt that "the nobles were changeable, unreliable and mercenary, and just as apt as pope or king to absorb for themselves what belonged to God."[38] Therefore, he wrote another letter, this time addressing the people of Scotland. In this letter, *A Letter Addressed to the Commonalty of Scotland*, he focused on the people's collective responsibility, stating that the people had the right and obligation to hold their rulers accountable and to rebel if necessary, under the condition that the rulers were idolatrous and unjust.

***

Now that we have introduced Knox's life in Geneva, the travel section that follows will take us to that internationally renowned city, which in the sixteenth century was known as the "Protestant Rome" under reformer Calvin's leadership.

---

37 Ibid.
38 John R. Gray, "The Political Theory of John Knox," *Church History* 8 (June 1939): 139.

Travel: Geneva, Switzerland

Situated where the River Rhone exits Lake Geneva, Geneva is a renowned international centre for finance and diplomacy. The city was established when the Romans came and conquered the place in the first century BC. An independent city-state in the sixteenth century, Geneva adopted Protestantism in 1536. The Reformation was initially led there by Guillaume Farel and then by John Calvin. Under Calvin's leadership, the city came to be known as the "Protestant Rome."

City of Geneva

When Knox came to Geneva in the 1550s, there were already many religious refugees in the city. In 1556, the year he accepted the call to be pastor of the English-exile church there, Protestant refugees already made up one-quarter of the city's population. Most of the refugees were French, but there were also Italians, Spanish, Dutch, Scots, and English. Knox's English congregation consisted of about 150 members who worshipped in the Church of Notre-Dame-la-Neuve.

Andy Kuo

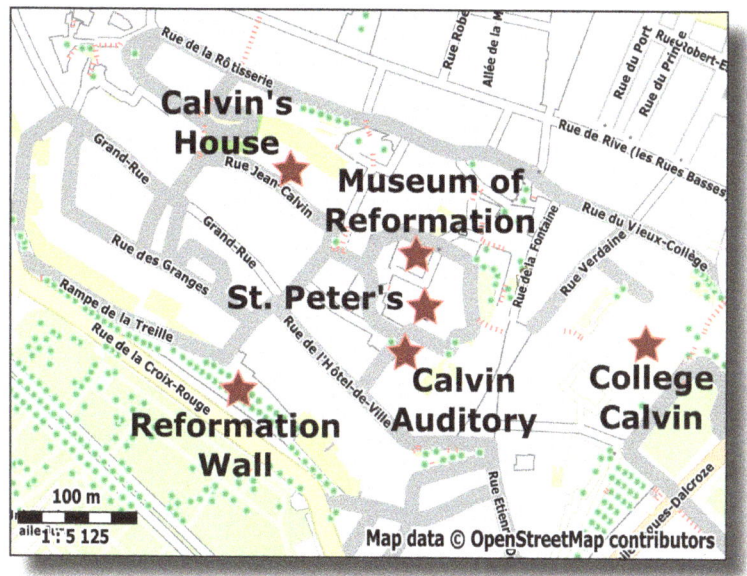

Map of Geneva's Old Town

St Peter's Cathedral

Standing on the hill of the old town of Geneva, the cathedral oversees the city. It was built between 1150 and 1250 on top of an ancient basilica that dates back to the sixth century. In 1397, the Chapel of Maccabee was added. Geneva's Reformation brought dramatic changes to the interior of the building. All the interior decoration and ornamentation were removed. The paintings were covered over.

St Peter's Cathedral

It was here that Calvin preached twice every Sunday and on weekdays, every other week. When Knox first arrived in Geneva to seek advice from Calvin in 1554, he likely also came here to worship and heard Calvin preaching in this magnificent church building.

Interior of St Peter's Cathedral

The sanctuary of the cathedral is plain, signifying the importance of the Protestant Reformation. A chair once used by Calvin is on display in the sanctuary. The Communion table at the front of the sanctuary was a gift from the Church of Scotland in 1950, a symbolism of the friendship between the Churches of Geneva and Scotland since the time of Knox and Calvin.

Calvin's chair

The Communion table: a gift from the Church of Scotland in 1950

Church of Notre-Dame-la-Neuve (Calvin Auditory)

The Calvin Auditory stands on an earlier tenth-century chapel. This Gothic chapel is built right next to St Peter's Cathedral. The auditory was known as Church of Notre-Dame-la-Neuve in Knox's time. When Knox was here, he was the pastor of the English congregation that worshipped in this location between 1556 and 1559. It was also in this location that the famous Geneva Bible was translated. Calvin's company of pastors also met in this location to discuss and make decisions regarding the affairs of the churches in Geneva. Today, there are still English, Dutch, and Italian congregations that worship here.

The door to Calvin Auditory

Calvin's House

On Rue Calvin, in the old city of Geneva, is the site where Protestant Reformer John Calvin lived. In the sixteenth century, the street was called Rue des Chanoines. However, the house where Calvin actually lived was demolished in 1706. Today, an encryption on the stone wall of the house marks the site where Calvin once resided.

When Knox first met Calvin in 1554, he was likely taken to this house. It was a noisy neighborhood, as refugees flooded the city. In the sixteenth century, at its peak, the refugee influx doubled the entire city's population. Calvin's house was also packed with friends and relatives. His two stepchildren, brother, sister-in-law, and their eight children all lived together with him.

At this site once stood the house where Calvin lived from 1543 to 1564. It was demolished in 1706, leaving only the plaque to commemorate the great reformer.

College Calvin

One of the key features of the Protestant Reformation was its emphasis on reading the Bible in one's own language. In order for any common people to read the Bible, they needed to be able to read. Education was the key to literacy. In 1559, Geneva's grammar school was established. Boys of the city were able to learn Latin, Greek, logic, rhetoric, the classics, and so forth. Study was intense: children attended schools for ten hours a day, six days a week, in the sixteenth century.

College Calvin

Geneva's emphasis on education likely influenced Knox's vision for education in Scotland. *The Book of Discipline*, which Knox helped to draft, also envisioned a nation with all its citizens able to read the Bible on their own. Unfortunately, the vision for universal education as outlined in *The Book of Discipline* was not realized in Knox's time.

The Academy

In addition to the grammar school, Calvin established the Academy to train ministers and pastors; they were then sent back to their home countries to spread the Reformation message. Knox was one of the students here. The Academy later came to be known as the University of Geneva.

The Reformation Wall

Standing against the old fortifications, below the City Hall and facing the University of Geneva, the Reformation Wall was commissioned in 1909 to commemorate the 400th anniversary of Calvin's birth and the 350th anniversary of the Academy of Calvin. The four large statutes, from left to right, are Guillaume Farel, Calvin, Theodore Beza, and Knox. Each of them was an important reformer in the sixteenth century. Surrounding the monument, six smaller statues depict sixteenth and seventeenth century reformers. Between the smaller statues are four reliefs illustrating the spread of the Reformed faith throughout Europe and America. Among them is a relief showing Knox preaching against Mary, Queen of Scots, at St Giles' Church.

From left to right: Guillaume Farel, John Calvin, Theodore Beza, and John Knox

In the Footsteps of John Knox

John Knox preaching against Mary, Queen of Scots, at St Giles' in Edinburgh

International Museum of the Reformation

The museum was founded in 2005 and showcases the history of Geneva's Reformation since 1536. Several versions of the original Bible translation and Calvin's *Institutes* are on display. Its multimedia room also features the Genevan Psalters sung by Protestants in the sixteenth century. Visitors can visit the audio room to listen to the Psalters. The building that housed the museum was built in the eighteenth-century on the former site of the Cathedral cloisters. This was the location where townspeople gathered in 1536, making the decision to adopt Protestantism.

International Museum of the Reformation
© Romano1246 / CC BY-SA 3.0.

Chapter 6: Back to Scotland

In November of 1558, Knox's second son, Eleazer, was born. Earlier in the year, on June 24, Knox and his good friend and co-minister Christopher Goodman were both granted citizenship in Geneva. He was happy and settled. However, a Scot named John Gray traveled to Geneva on his way to Rome and delivered letters from Lord James Stewart, the Earl of Glencairn, and other Protestant leaders.

The situation in Scotland appeared very different from when Knox was invited one year before. Mary, Queen of Scots, had married the son of King Henry II in France on April 24. Many in Scotland were concerned, fearing that the King of France and his court would exercise political influence in Scotland. Only four days later, Walter Milne, a former priest and Protestant advocate, was burned at the stake in St Andrews. There was great fear that a nationwide Protestant persecution was imminent. Tension between Catholics and Protestants was becoming acute. The Protestant nobles were inviting Knox back to lead the Reformation.

Knox was reluctant. Not only had his second son just been born, but he and Goodman had been elected as pastors of the English congregation for the following year. Knowing that Knox could be hard to persuade, the Protestant nobles also wrote to Calvin, hoping that Calvin would convince Knox to return. Calvin did encourage Knox to return, as he thought that Reformation work in Scotland would be more important than any other task Knox might undertake. Knox finally agreed, and he began his travel on January 28, 1559, to the port of Dieppe.

When he arrived at Dieppe on February 19, he wrote at once to England for safe conduct. It would have been easier to cross the English Channel and travel through England than travel all the way to

Scotland by sea. That way, Knox could also visit friends in London and Northumberland on his way to Scotland. However, the request was refused twice; Queen Elizabeth was still infuriated by Knox's book, *The First Blast of the Trumpet*. Knox also wrote twice to William Cecil, Elizabeth's secretary of state, but received no reply. By the end of April, realizing that safe conduct would not be granted, he set off to Scotland by sea.

The Sermon at Perth

On May 2, 1559, Knox was back in Scotland. The queen regent, not knowing that Knox had landed, summoned Protestant preachers Paul Methven, John Willock, William Harlaw, and John Christison to appear before the court on May 10. She planned to outlaw and banish them. The Protestant nobles tried to persuade the queen regent not to go forward with such a plan, but she proved indifferent. They then decided to accompany the preachers to Stirling. First, they would gather and assemble at Perth (known as St Johnstoun in the sixteenth century). Knox quickly rode over and joined them. Having heard that the Protestant nobles had gathered, the queen regent softened her strategy. She postponed the summoning indefinitely. While some Protestants were suspicious, others were convinced that she had changed her mind. Many returned to their homes. The queen then summoned the preachers again without giving them time to travel, and they were outlawed for nonappearance.

Knox interpreted the development of these events as the regent's inherent duplicity. On May 11, in the parish church of St John, Knox preached a sermon "vehement against idolatry." Shortly after this sermon, a local priest entered the church to prepare for Mass. A boy challenged the priest and shouted, "This is intolerable, that when God by his Word hath plainly damned idolatry, we shall stand and see it used in despite."[39] The priest cuffed him. The boy threw a stone but missed the priest. Instead, it hit a statue close to the tabernacle.

Some other people who had heard Knox's sermon were still in the parish building. They began to throw stones and smash images and statues in the church. People nearby, hearing the smashing sounds, came and joined in. When there were no more statues left to destroy, they ran to several friaries in the burgh, including the Grey and Black Friaries and the Charterhouse. They attacked and destroyed all the statues and images they saw along the way.

---

39   Knox, *The History of the Reformation of Religion in Scotland*, 114.

When the regent heard about the event in Perth, she gathered her troops and marched to Perth. It had been a tactical mistake by the Protestants, as it left the Protestant nobles wrong-footed. They negotiated with the queen regent and allowed her and her royal guards to enter the city to demonstrate her authority. On May 30, 1559, Knox preached a final sermon at St John's Church. Afterward, the Protestants left the city, and Mary of Guise and her troops entered it. She dismissed the Protestant Provost Lord Ruthven and garrisoned the burgh with four hundred troops.

Reforming St Andrews

Since the event at Perth led to occupation by royal troops, the Protestant movements needed to regain momentum. Led by two young nobles, Earl of Argyll and Lord James Stewarts, the Protestants named themselves Lords of the Congregation. They aimed to bring reform to Scotland's ecclesiastical capital, St Andrews.

The news of Knox's return to St Andrews reached Roman Catholic Archbishop Hamilton, whose seat was in St Andrews Cathedral. The archbishop threatened that if Knox preached at the cathedral, "a dozen culverings [guns] should light upon his nose."[40] Fearing for Knox's safety, the Protestant nobles tried to dissuade him from entering the town. However, he was adamant. He would not let this opportunity slip away, for when he had lain sick on the French galley, he had declared that one day he would come back and preach again. Fearlessly, he entered St Andrews and preached at Holy Trinity Church on Sunday, June 11. For the sermon, Knox chose the theme of Christ cleansing the temple in Jerusalem. He urged Christians to cleanse the church. That same week, images and wooden statues were taken from the local churches and burned outside Deans Court, the location where Milne had been burned at the stake. In a letter that Knox wrote to his friend Anna Locke in England, he reflected upon his experiences of the past forty days or more, stating, "The long thirst of my wretched heart is satisfied in abundance…God used my tongue in my native country, to the manifestation of his glory."[41]

---

40 Quoted in Dawson, *John Knox*, 181.
41 Knox, *The Works of John Knox*, VI:26.

The Confrontation at Cuparmuir

Realizing that he had lost St Andrews, Archbishop Hamilton fled to Falkland Palace to seek the queen regent's help. She ordered the French commander, the Duke of Chatelherault, along with French Ambassador Henri Cleutin, to lead the French troop to Cupar, a strategic crossing six miles from St Andrews. Upon hearing the news, the Lords of the Congregation marched out quickly from St Andrews to confront the enemy. This was a crucial moment. One of the Lords of the Congregation was anxious to mediate. He rode to see the French commander and ambassador. The French commander was willing to comply, but the ambassador balked. After the ambassador climbed the Hill of Tarvit and saw the much greater size of the Protestant army, he agreed to come to terms. It was agreed that the French and their artillery would withdraw and that the Protestants would disband their army.

As the summer progressed, the Lords of the Congregation continued to push forward. They retook the city of Perth. Then they took the city of Stirling and reached Edinburgh, the capital of Scotland, in June of 1559. The queen regent fled to Dunbar to avoid being trapped at the capital city. She ordered the Protestants to leave Edinburgh, but her order was refused. On July 7, Knox was elected as the minister of St Giles' Church, the largest church in the capital. It was a triumphal moment for Knox and the Protestants. However, they soon realized that they had overextended themselves. It was just a matter of time until Mary of Guise's reinforcements from France would arrive. They knew that they still had a tough battle ahead of them.

The Lords of the Congregation figured that they needed to plead for assistance from England. Knox also contacted his friends in England to request aid. In addition, he contacted his former congregation in Geneva to make collections to support the Scottish Protestant movement. The Lords of the Congregation even appointed Knox as a diplomat to negotiate with the English. England faced a dilemma. On one hand, they did not want to see Scotland absorbed as a satellite state of France. On the other hand, they had already made peace with the French with the Treaty of Cateau-Cambresis. Any negotiations had to be done secretly. By late autumn, knowing his own limitation as a diplomat, Knox was relieved to hear that William Maitland of Lethington would lead the negotiations.

By then, Knox had retreated back to St Andrews. His wife Marjorie, two sons, and mother-in-law had come to St Andrews on September 20, 1559. It was in the autumn of 1559 in St Andrews that Knox was able to start writing his famous *History of the Reformation of Religion within the Realm of Scotland*.

During these struggles, Knox's preaching proved decisive. His stirring rhetoric greatly motivated the Protestant soldiers. When faced with defeat, Knox interpreted the consequence as a lack of faith in God. In a letter to Anne Locke, he wrote, "We trusted too much…in our own strength."[42] The only way out was to completely rely on God. He was able to motivate the soldiers by encouraging them that God was on their side and that any adversary was God's test of them. His sermons were like having five hundred trumpets blowing in one's ears.[43] When the Protestants suffered a great defeat in early November, and Mary of Guise retook Edinburgh, Knox rode to Stirling to encourage the Protestants. On November 8, 1559, he preached a powerful sermon in the Church of the Holy Rude. Using Psalm 80, he encouraged the Protestants to trust in God, not any other men on earth. His sermon served as a great reminder and boosted the Protestants' morale.

In January of 1560, the Protestants were losing ground. The queen regent's troops had been moving through Fife, raiding the countryside and burning the houses of Protestant lairds. As they moved to within six miles of St Andrews, people in the town were desperate. It was at this point that the tide turned. The English reinforcements arrived by sea, forcing the French to retreat. To Knox, it was God's merciful providence. He wrote with gratitude, "We have had wonderful experience of God's merciful providence."[44]

By April, other English reinforcements marched in. Meanwhile, the queen regent, Mary of Guise, became seriously ill. She eventually died on June 11, 1560. After her death, the French, English, and Protestant Lords negotiated to end the war. Both the French and English armies were to withdraw from Scotland. After the treaty, a great service of thanksgiving was held at St Giles' in Edinburgh. In the service, Knox prayed with thanksgiving that God had "partly removed

---

42 Ibid., VI:100.
43 Randolph to Cecil, 7 September 1561, *Calendar of State Papers relating to Scotland and Mary, Queen of Scots 1547–1603*, ed. J. Bain *et al.*, 13 vols (London: HMSO, 1898–1969), vol. I, no. 1017.
44 Knox, *The Works of John Knox*, VI:108.

our darkness, suppressed idolatry and taken from above our heads the devouring sword of merciless strangers."[45] In his sermon, he encouraged the congregation that "we must now forget ourselves and bear the barrow to build the houses of God."[46] In the summer of 1560, the Parliament passed a series of acts of reform. Scotland had become a Protestant nation.

The military and diplomatic victory in the summer of 1560 had ensured these acts of reform. Now, many Protestants were glad that the conflict was finally over, but Knox knew that there was more work to be done. To implement Protestantism across Scotland, a system of church governance and a national confession of faith would be necessary. Thus we now come to introduce two important documents that Knox helped draft: *The First Book of Discipline* and *The Scots Confession*.

The First Book of Discipline

In the previous spring, Knox and five other ministers, all of whom were named John, began drafting an important document, *The First Book of Discipline*. The book adopted the Continental Reformed model of church offices. The entire country was to be divided into dioceses. Instead of having a bishop in each diocese, a superintendent was appointed to assist vacant churches and to plant churches. The book also categorized the different kinds of offenses to be regulated by the church (such as inappropriate clothing or language, unethical business practices, and oppressing the poor) or by the state (such as blasphemy, adultery, murder, and perjury). It also outlined the procedures for excommunication. One visionary intent of the book was the call for universal education for all children, regardless of their economic status. The goal was to give children sufficient education to be able to read, learn the catechism, and understand the basics of Latin.

On January 27, 1561, the Parliament approved *The First Book of Discipline* in the Tolbooth of Edinburgh. However, implementing this large-scale change to a nation was a daunting task. In fact, Knox did not live to see the full implementation of ecclesiastical structure across the nation. Finding the financial resources to fund universal education became a huge burden. Even fifty years later, the Parliament was still trying to fund schools in every parish.

---

45 Knox, *The History of the Reformation of Religion in Scotland*, 205.
46 Ibid., 206.

The Scots Confession

Like *The Book of Discipline*, *The Scots Confession* was composed by the "six Johns." It was the official statement of faith for the Protestant Church in Scotland until the *Westminster Confession* of 1647. The *Confession* was based on the Reformation principle that all doctrines are based on Scripture. It begins with a preface urging the readers to contact the authors if they thought they found anything that was contrary to Scripture. It is worth noting that the idea of resistance against tyranny had found its place in this *Confession*. In Article 14, in which the *Confession* discusses the sixth commandment "You shall not murder," the book states that one is "to repress tyranny."[47]

***

In the travel section that follows, we will visit the historical town of Perth set beside the beautiful River Tay. It was here, at St John's Kirk, where the Protestant Reformation was sparked. The royal stronghold city of Stirling, and Edinburgh, the capital city of Scotland, will be introduced to the reader in the travel section after chapters 7 and 8, respectively.

---

47 G. D Henderson, *The Scots Confession, 1560* (Edinburgh: Saint Andrew Press, 1960), 68.

Travel: Perth

Perth is located on the banks of the River Tay. By the sixteenth century, the city was also known as "St John's Toun" or "St Johnstoun" because at the center of the burgh stood the church dedicated to St John the Baptist, known as St John's Kirk. Since Scottish writer Sir Walter Scott wrote the story "Fair Maid of Perth" in 1828, the city is also known as "The Fair City."

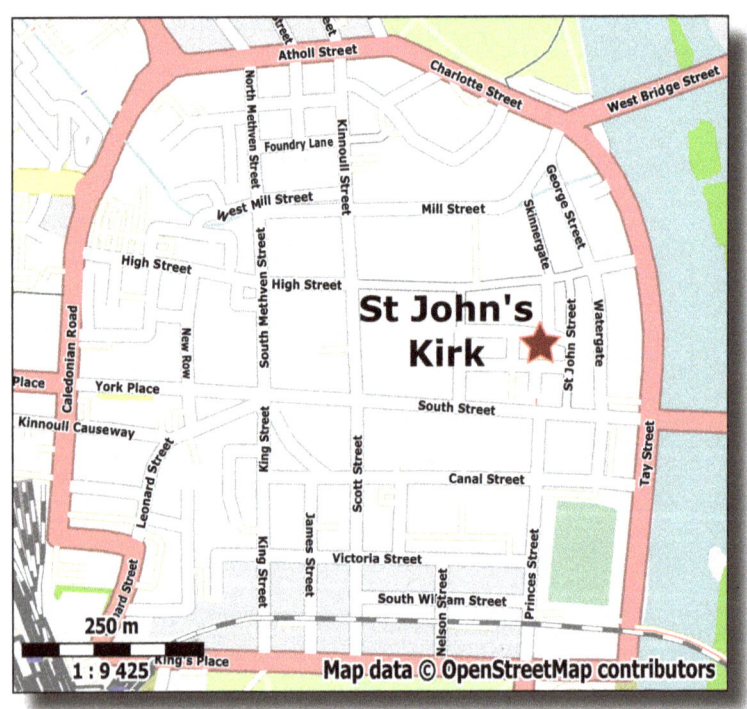

Map of Perth

River Tay running through Perth
© Lis Burke / CC BY-SA 2.0.

St John's Kirk

St John's Kirk is the oldest building still standing in Perth. The main structural elements of the church were built between 1440 and 1500. The church tower and lead-clad spire is still the main landmark in Perth today.

When Knox returned to Scotland in 1559, he came to Perth to meet with Protestant supporters. On Sunday, May 11, he preached a fiery sermon against idolatry in St John's Kirk. Later, a priest struck a boy who objected to him. In retaliation, the boy threw a stone at the priest but missed. Instead, the stone hit one of the statues on the altar. This incited those who were still in the church to begin smashing statues. Soon, people outside the church joined and destroyed many statues and icons in monasteries within Perth.

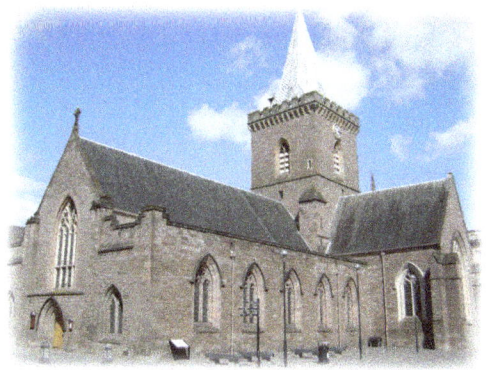

St John's Kirk, Perth
© Kilnburn / Wikimedia Commons.

Chapter 7: Mary, Queen of Scots

I fear the preaching and prayers of John Knox more than any army or navy the world might launch.

—Mary, Queen of Scots

Toward the end of 1560, Knox's wife Marjorie died. In her last hours, she gave her two little sons blessings and prayed that they would always be true worshippers of God. Losing his deep love, Knox mourned greatly. A few months later Calvin sent his condolences, saying, "You found a wife whose like is not found everywhere."[48] Calvin also wrote to Knox's good companion, Christopher Goodman, to ask him to bring Knox comfort.

Shortly after Marjorie's death, news from France arrived that Francis II, the husband of Mary, Queen of Scots, had died in December. After his death, Mary was no longer the queen of France. It made no sense for her to continue to stay in France. Therefore, she decided to return to Scotland. In August 1561, her galley sailed into Leith, and she was escorted to Holyrood Palace.

Having experienced the regime of Catholic Queen Mary Tudor in England, Knox was highly suspicious of Mary, Queen of Scots, as she was also a Roman Catholic. He feared that a new round of persecution might be imminent. For Knox, when it came to religious matters, nothing could be negotiated. In an attempt to show Mary their Protestant strength, Knox gathered a group of Protestant supporters and some musicians, and they stood outside the palace and sang Protestant metrical psalms.

---

48 Knox, *The Works of John Knox*, VI:124.

On the first Sunday after Mary returned, Mass was said at the Chapel Royal at Holyrood Palace. The furious Knox preached a sermon against the queen and her idolatrous practice on the same Sunday and the following Sunday. He was concerned that many people would join Mary and attend Mass instead. In the sermons, he reminded the Protestants that their recent victory had come because of their complete reliance on God.

Summoned to Mary's Court

During Mary's reign in Scotland, Knox remained skeptical of her Roman Catholic faith. He often preached against her attending Mass. On one occasion, he even preached against her love of dancing. On the issue of her marriage, he preached bluntly that she should not marry any Roman Catholic at all. He was concerned that Scotland might experience the same fate as England during Mary Tudor's reign. Mary, having read Knox's *The First Blast*, did not like Knox's view on women ruling nations or his active resistance against idolatrous rulers.

This mistrust between Knox and Mary led to Mary summoning Knox to the court several times. The only record that we have is Knox's own account of the event, in which he portrayed himself as a brave person to confront Mary, Queen of Scots. After one of the meetings, as Knox left the palace, some courtiers inquired why he was fearless. He answered, "Why should the pleasing face of a gentlewoman fear me? I have looked in the faces of many angry men and yet have not been afraid above measure."[49] Knox's bold and strong attitude often made meetings with Mary unpleasant. There were occasions when the queen was offended, stayed silent for several minutes, or even burst into tears, as recorded by Knox.

The final meeting between Knox and Mary was in 1563. Knox was charged with treason and appeared before the Privy Council. Mary and her courtiers tried to make a case that Knox was supporting Protestant authorities to prosecute those who attended Mass. However, the Privy Council rejected the charge, as Knox was simply supporting the authorities who followed the law passed by Parliament. After this final meeting, Knox and Mary would never see each other face-to-face again. However, Knox managed to infuriate the queen on many different occasions, especially when he was behind the pulpit.

---

49 Knox, *The History of the Reformation of Religion in Scotland*, 271.

A Married Man Again

By now, Knox was nearly fifty years old. In the spring of 1564, he was married again, this time to Margaret Stewart, the daughter of his old friend Lord Ochiltree. She was only seventeen. It was likely a marriage of convenience, as he was aging and his two sons were still young.[50] Mary, Queen of Scots, was furious, as Margaret was a member of Scotland's royal house.

Raised in the Protestant faith, Margaret was well educated and she acted as Knox's secretary. The couple had a vibrant social life. They enjoyed suppers with Protestant leaders and nobles at their home. Margaret bore him three daughters: Martha, Margaret, and Elizabeth.

The Fall of Mary, Queen of Scots

After Mary, Queen of Scots, returned to Scotland, her marriage was the concern of the entire nation. In the sixteenth century, a royal marriage was not one of pure love. It needed to be politically calculated to bring maximum benefit to one's kingdom. The religion of any future husband for Mary was also a concern of the Protestant nobles. Initially, there were discussions about the possibility of Mary entering a marriage arrangement with the Catholic Prince Philip II of Spain. Fortunately for the Protestants, the marriage did not work out. In the end, Mary chose Englishman Lord Darnley instead.

Darnley's father was in the line of succession to the throne of Scotland, while his mother was in the line of succession to the throne of England, second only to Mary. The marriage would strengthen the couple's claim to the thrones of both England and Scotland. When Darnley traveled from England to Scotland, Mary quickly fell in love with him. They were married on July 29, 1565.

On August 16, Lord Darnley went to attend a service at St Giles'. Knox deliberately preached a sermon from the Old Testament regarding the story of King Ahab and Queen Jezebel. He referred to Jezebel as "that harlot Jezebel," and everyone in the congregation knew to whom he was referring. Lord Darnley was furious and refused to eat dinner that day. Knox may have had every reason to preach from that

---

50 Marshall, *John Knox*, chap. 14.

text, but it was obvious that he went too far. Even though he had the strong support of the council of Edinburgh to preach at St Giles', he was banned from preaching for fifteen or twenty days.[51] For the Protestant nobles who supported him, it was an embarrassment before the queen. Knox's charismatic preaching and his strong faith in God had been great assets at the time of rebellion in 1559 and 1560, but his boldness often become a liability in court politics.

After the marriage, Lord Darnley was disappointed that Mary did not grant him the crown matrimonial (the right to rule as a King if Mary were to die before him). He was also jealous of Mary's secretary, David Riccio, as Mary's possible lover and perhaps the one who had advised the queen not to grant him the crown matrimonial. Darnley and other nobles hatched a plot to murder Riccio, and Riccio was eventually murdered in March of 1565. Mary was briefly frightened but quickly calmed down and used her skills to convince Darnley to switch back to her side. The other conspirators had to flee, fearing that Darnley would tell her who else was involved. Knox did not take part in the assassination, but he likely knew of the plot beforehand.[52] It was therefore dangerous for Knox to continue to stay in Edinburgh. He fled to Ayrshire. It appeared as though this would be another exile. He greatly feared that Scotland would become Catholic again.

In the spring of 1566, he contemplated where he should go next. At one point, he thought to join his former colleague Christopher Goodman, from Geneva's English congregation, on Goodman's mission to Ireland. This did not work out. He eventually traveled to England, where he would meet with many of his old friends from his years of exile in England and Geneva.

Meanwhile in Scotland, Mary's reign took a dramatic turn. In February of 1567, Lord Darnley was mysteriously murdered. Many thought that Lord Bothwell was involved. He was arrested and tried but acquitted due to lack of evidence. On May 15, Bothwell and Mary were married at Holyrood Palace. It was too much for the Protestant lords; they raised an army against Mary and Bothwell. Mary eventually surrendered and was imprisoned in Lochleven Castle. In July, she was forced to abdicate her throne and handed over her kingdom to her one-year-old son, James VI.

---

51 Ibid.
52 Dawson, *John Knox*, 250.

In the Footsteps of John Knox

***

In the travel section, we will take you to Scotland's royal stronghold, the city of Stirling. It was here that many royal events took place in the sixteenth century, including the coronations of Mary, Queen of Scots, James V, and James VI. It was also here that Knox preached a powerful sermon that boosted the morale of Protestant forces during the 1559–1560 struggle against the forces of the queen regent, Mary of Guise.

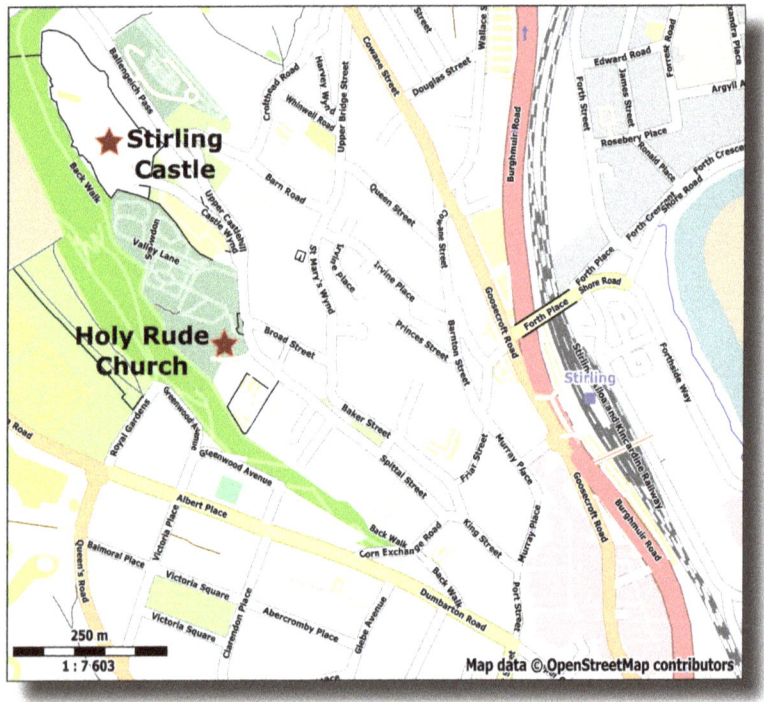

Map of Stirling

Travel: Stirling

There is a saying that "he who holds Stirling holds Scotland," emphasizing the importance of Stirling to Scotland. Stirling was once the Scottish capital; its location is strategically important, overlooking the River Forth that divides the Lowlands from the Highlands. The old town is situated along a long, narrow, steep hill. It is like a "mini-Edinburgh," with a steep path leading to Stirling Castle.

Surroundings of Stirling
© Janfrie1988 / Wikimedia Commons.

Church of Holy Rude

Founded in 1129 during the reign of David I, the Church of the Holy Rude is the second oldest building in Stirling, after the castle. The phrase "Holy Rude" means Holy Cross. It served as the parish church for the burgh of Stirling. Because the church is closely related to Stirling Castle, it had the support and patronage of the royal house of Stewart between the fifteenth and seventeenth century. Today, it is the only active church other than Westminster Abbey to have held a coronation in Britain.

A view of Holy Rude Church from Stirling Castle
© Postdlf / CC BY-SA 3.0.

During the conflict between the Lords of the Congregation and the force of the queen regent, Mary of Guise, when the Lords of the Congregation were at their lowest point, Knox preached a powerful sermon here that helped boost the morale of their forces. In the sermon, Knox preached from Psalm 80; the text referred to the metaphor of God rooting out the heathen, planting a great vine, and then seeing it destroyed. Knox said to the people that here were two groups: one that trusted in God completely and another that trusted God only half-heartedly. He told them that this was God's test, and the solution was to simply turn to God and rely on God instead of any men. His powerful words eventually restored the confidence of the Protestant force.

After Mary, Queen of Scots, was forced to abdicate her throne, the coronation of her thirteen-month-old son King James VI was held in this church on July 29, 1567. Knox came from Edinburgh to preach the sermon. In the sermon, he preached about the crowning of the young

King Joash and how Joash trusted in God with the help of the priest, Johoida, to act against the wicked Queen Athaliah. It is worth noting that the order of the coronation was unconventional at the time. It followed the recommendation of the General Assembly's Articles to have the oath taken (by the Earl of Morton on James's behalf) before the coronation. The oath symbolized the contract made between the monarchy and the people. The divine right to rule as symbolized in the coronation could only be granted after the oath. The change thus emphasized the contractual nature of the bond between the monarchy and people.[53]

Interior of Holy Rude Church
© RonAlmog / CC BY-SA 2.5.

Stirling Castle

Located atop the hill that overlooks the primary passage between the Lowlands and the Highlands, the castle is historically one of the most important castles in Scotland. It was built in the twelfth century by King David I. In the sixteenth century, it underwent significant changes, as the Great Hall, Royal Palace, and Chapel Royal were added. The castle witnessed several important coronations, including that of infant James V in 1513, and Mary, Queen of Scots, in 1543. Mary's son, the future King James VI, was baptized here in 1566.

Aerial view of the castle
© Andrew Shiva / CC BY-SA 4.0.

---

53 Ibid., 271–72.

A reconstruction of the Great Hall
© Kilburn. Free to distribute or use.

Interior of Chapel Royal
© Janfrie1988 / Wikimedia Commons.

Chapter 8: Knox's Final Years

Knox returned to Scotland in June 1567 after the arrest of Mary, Queen of Scots. He continued to preach against Mary and demanded that she be executed, as Knox could not help but associate her with the second Mary Tudor of England. His sermons for the summer of 1567 all focused on 2 Chronicles and 2 Kings from the Old Testament. Like the kings and queens in the Old Testament, he felt that Scotland's monarchs also had the responsibility to keep covenant with God.

In December 1567, Knox was invited to preach at the opening of the Scottish Parliament. He witnessed the Parliament ratifying all the acts of 1560 in favor of the Reformed Church and the confirmation of Mary's abdication and accusation of having been involved in the murder of her husband, Lord Darnley. The following spring, on May 2, 1568, Mary escaped from Lochleven Castle. She gathered her supporters and marched against Regent Moray. Her army was eventually defeated. She fled to England but was placed under house arrest by her cousin Elizabeth.

Peace did not last long. In early 1570, Regent Moray was assassinated after a plot planned by Archbishop John Hamilton. Even though Knox and Moray often had different opinions, Knox was horrified to hear the news. He mourned the loss of Scotland's Regent, and the assassination propelled the country into an open civil war.

Meanwhile, Knox's health was declining fast. Although he had suffered from severe headaches, fevers, and digestive problems since his time in the French galley, he had remained actively involved in ministerial activities. In October of 1570, Knox suffered a mild stroke. As a result of the stroke, he lost his speech, and his left side was weakened. He would need a stick in his right hand and would require assistance.

In the spring of 1571, the king's supporters captured Dumbarton Castle and arrested Archbishop Hamilton. He was hanged at Stirling on April 7, 1571. His supporters vowed retaliation and openly threatened Knox's life. A few evenings later, a shot was fired at a window of his house. Fortunately, he was unharmed. As the situation in Edinburgh worsened, it was deemed unsafe for Knox to continue to stay. At first, he refused to leave Edinburgh. After some persuasion from his colleagues, he and his family finally left the city in July and traveled to St Andrews.

At St Andrews

After Knox and his family arrived at St Andrews, they stayed at a house near St Leonard's College. Even though his health continued to deteriorate, he still preached at the Holy Trinity Church in St Andrews. The fifteen-year-old student James Melville, who was studying at St Andrews at that time, recorded his observation of Knox's preaching. His secretary, Bannatyne, would support Knox on the left side with a hand under his armpit. Once they came to the church, Bannatyne and others would lift Knox into the pulpit. As Knox preached, he leaned heavily on the pulpit. He would speak quietly for about half an hour. When he moved on to application, he would become animated as if he would shatter the pulpit to demonstrate his point.[54]

During his other days, he got up usually only once a week. When he was feeling better, he might go to the gardens of St Leonard's College. Sometimes, he might call students over and give them blessings. Melville felt that the greatest benefit that he received while in St Andrews was the opportunity of seeing "that extraordinary man of God, Mr. John Knox."[55]

On July 31, 1572, the civil war ended in a truce. Knox received messages from some of the members of the congregation of St Giles', inviting him to come back to Edinburgh. He left St Andrews on August 17 and traveled to the southern coast of Fife and across the Forth to Leith. When he preached at St Giles' on August 31, his voice was so weak that it was difficult for the entire congregation to hear him. As a result, it was arranged for him to preach in a smaller space. He chose

---

54 J. Melville, *The Autobiography and Diary of Mr James Melville, Minister of Kilrenny in Fife*, ed. R. Pitcairn (Edinburgh: Wodrow Society, 1842), 26, 33.
55 Quoted in Marshall, *John Knox*, chap. 15.

his final set of sermons to expound upon the history of the Passion of Christ. Despite his weak voice, he was still preaching with burning zeal.

Final Weeks

By November, Knox's health was fading fast. The elders and deacons of the church came to see him on November 17. He charged them to hold on to their faith and walk in the path of righteousness. In the following few days, his friends, including the Protestant nobles, came to say farewell.

In the final week before his death, his wife and ministerial colleagues took turns reading different Scripture passages as well as the "Prayer for the Sick" and Calvin's commentary. On Monday, November 24, around midday, he called his wife Margaret to read 1 Corinthians 15 on the meaning of Christ's resurrection. At about five o'clock in the afternoon, he told Margaret to "go read where I cast my first anchor."[56] His wife understood perfectly that he meant John 17, in which Jesus told God that he had preached in this world and even though he was hated, God should keep them from evil so that they might all be united one day in glory.

Shortly after ten o'clock in the evening, his family and friends conducted the usual evening prayers. When asked if he had heard the psalm singing and prayers, Knox replied, "I would to God that ye and all men heard them as I have heard them, and I praise God of that heavenly sound."[57] At about eleven o'clock, Robert Campbell heard Knox say, "Now it is done." When asked by Bannatyne to show that he remembered Christ's promises, Knox raised his hand and "slept away without any pain."[58] He had gone home to glory. Knox's funeral was held two days later at St Giles' Church. The Earl of Morton delivered the eulogy: "There lies he who never feared nor flattered any flesh."[59]

***

In the final travel section of the book, we will visit the Firth of Forth's southern shore and the capital city of Edinburgh. We will visit the

---

56 Knox, *The Works of John Knox*, VI:643.
57 Ibid.
58 Ibid., VI:644.
59 Melville, *The Autobiography and Diary of Mr James Melville, Minister of Kilrenny in Fife*, 47.

Holyrood Palace, where Knox was summoned by Mary, Queen of Scots, as well as the John Knox House, where Knox was believed to have spent the last few months of his life. We will also explore Edinburgh Castle, where Mary gave birth to James VI, the future king of Scotland, and St Giles' Church, where Knox was the minister from the 1560s until his death.

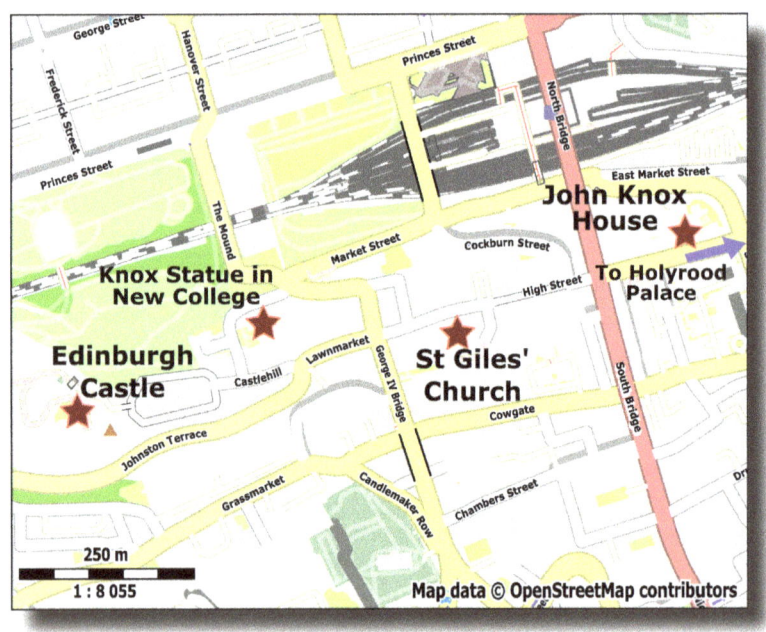

Map of Edinburgh's Old Town

Travel: Edinburgh

Edinburgh is the capital city and the second most populous city in Scotland. The city is located in Lothian on the Firth of Forth's southern shore. The city can be divided into the Old Town (before the 1700s) and the New Town (from the 1700s). During Scotland's Reformation, many important historical events happened in this city. A walk on the streets of the Old City will reveal these important historical sites: the palace where reformer John Knox was summoned by Mary, Queen of Scots; the church where Knox preached; and the castle where the son of Mary, Queen of Scots, was born.

Old Town of Edinburgh
© Ronnie Macdonald / CC BY-SA 2.0.

John Knox's Plaque

Knox served as the minister of St Giles' Church in the 1560s. Between 1560 to 1566, Knox and his family stayed at the manse near Warriston's Close on High Street. Today, a memorial plaque with the inscription "Near this Spot Stood the Manse in which Lived John Knox 1560–1566" is placed on the wall near the spot where he and his family once lived.

The plaque showing the manse where John Knox lived
© Kim Traynor / CC BY-SA 3.0.

Holyrood Palace

Located at the bottom of the Royal Mile in Edinburgh, the palace is at the Mile's opposite end from Edinburgh Castle. It was built on the site of a monastery founded in 1128 by King David I. The palace served as the principal residence of the Scottish monarchy. It is currently the official royal residence of Queen Elizabeth II when she visits Scotland.

Holyrood Palace
© Kim Traynor / CC BY-SA 3.0.

On the first night when Mary, Queen of Scots, returned to Scotland in 1561, she stayed in this royal palace. In an attempt to demonstrate to the Catholic queen the Protestant strength in Scotland, Knox led a group of Protestants in singing metrical Psalms outside the palace.

It was also here that Knox was summoned by Mary, Queen of Scots, to discuss religious matters in Scotland. The dramatic scenes as recorded by Knox were fascinating. Knox's strong and bold attitude and his confrontational style managed to upset the queen, and there were occasions when the queen burst into tears or stayed silent for several minutes.

St Giles' Church

Located between Edinburgh Castle and Holyrood Palace, St Giles' Church is the principal place of worship of the Church of Scotland. It can be seen as Scotland's Westminster Abbey, containing nearly two hundred memorials honoring distinctive Scots through the ages. It is also often said to be the Mother Church of Presbyterianism, due to its significance in Scotland's Reformation history.

St Giles' Church
© Carlos Delgado / CC BY-SA 3.0.

The church is a gigantic Gothic building, and most of the present structure was built in the fourteenth century, including the present nave, transepts, chancels, and the four great pillars. Side chapels were added gradually over the next 150 years. By the middle of the sixteenth century, there were about fifty side altars.

In the Footsteps of John Knox

Interior of St Giles'
© Evans Traynor / CC BY-SA 3.0.

Scotland's Reformation brought significant changes to the church. The reformer Knox was elected as minister in 1559 and served here until his death in 1572. Even though the church underwent significant interior changes, they were not as dramatic and violent as those of many other Reformation cities in Europe. Edinburgh's city records show that it took over a year to convert St Giles' to Protestant worship.[60]

Toward the end of the sixteenth century, as the population of Edinburgh continued to grow, the town council decided to divide the church into four congregations. The building was divided by stone walls to form four separate churches. People were supposed to go to their church based on their home's geographic location. However, it was often the case that people would go to their preferred church, depending on the style of preaching of the minister. It was not until the late nineteenth century that the internal walls were removed.

John Knox's Burial Spot

Knox died in Edinburgh on November 24, 1572 and was buried in St Giles' graveyard. Today, the graveyard surrounding St Giles' Church has been converted into parking lots. Knox's approximate burial site was located under parking space 23. The inscription on the plaque in

---

60 "The Scottish Reformation," accessed November 26, 2016, http://www.stgilescathedral.org.uk/saint-giles-history/scottish-reformation.

this parking space reads: "The above stone marks the approximate site of the burial in St Giles graveyard of John Knox, the great Scottish divine who died 24 Nov 1572."

John Knox's burial spot
© Kim Traynor / CC BY-SA 3.0.

John Knox Statue

A six-foot-tall statue of Knox located inside the church commemorates Scotland's reformer. It was cast in 1904 by the sculptor Pittendrigh MacGillivray and originally erected in Parliament Square.. The statue shows Knox's hand pointing to the Bible, signifying the importance of God's Word in our lives.

Statue of John Knox in St Giles'
© Ruth Chueh

In the Footsteps of John Knox

Stained-Glass Window of John Knox Preaching at St Giles'

Right next to the organ is a small chapel. The stained glass window above shows the dramatic scene of crowds gathered and listening to Knox preaching in St Giles' Church. His hand is on the Bible as he preaches to the congregation.

Knox preaching in St Giles'
© Kim Traynor / CC BY-SA 3.0.

John Knox Statue, New College

Located in New College, University of Edinburgh, is a statue of Knox. It stands at the quadrangle. The bronze statue was designed by John Hutchison and was erected in 1896. It depicts Knox in his gown, preaching with a Bible in his left hand. His right arm is raised toward heaven.

The inscription reads: "John Knox 1514–72. Erected by Scotsmen Who are Mindful of the Benefits Conferred by John Knox on Their Native Land. 1896."

Statue of John Knox in the New College quadrangle
© Stephencdickson / CC BY-SA 3.0.

Edinburgh Castle

Located on a hilltop, the castle dominates the skyline of Edinburgh. The home of Scotland's monarchy for centuries, the castle has witnessed royal births, medieval pageantry, and military sieges.

In Knox's time, during the struggles between the queen regent, Mary of Guise, and the Lords of the Congregations, Edinburgh Castle served as an important refuge for the queen regent, who died here in 1560 due to illness.

When Mary, Queen of Scots, returned to England, she held a procession to meet her people between Edinburgh Castle and Holyrood Palace through the Royal Mile. After her secretary, David Rizzio, was murdered in 1566, she moved to Edinburgh Castle for security reasons. It was here in June of 1566 that she bore her son James, the future King of Scotland and England. The Birth Chamber (also known as Mary's Room) is located in the Royal Palace building.

Royal Palace building where King James VI was born
© Christian Bickel / CC BY-SA 2.0.

After Mary, Queen of Scots, was forced to abdicate her throne, a group of her supporters known as the "Queen's Men" seized the castle in 1571. Protestants besieged the castle (this was known as the "Lang Siege") for two years.

John Knox House

The house dates back to 1470 and is the only medieval building surviving on the Royal Mile. Some believe that Knox stayed here, after he moved back to Edinburgh from St Andrews in 1572, until his death.[61] It is currently a museum of John Knox. The museum contains valuable information on Knox's life. The owner of the house in Knox's time, James Mossman—and his involvement in supporting Mary, Queen of Scots, in the attempt to restore Mary's throne—is also featured.

John Knox House
© Tony Hisgett / CC BY-SA 2.0.

---

61 Dawson, *John Knox*, 306

Bibliography

Bain J. et al. *Calendar of State Papers relating to Scotland and Mary, Queen of Scots 1547–1603*, ed. J. Bain et al., 13 vols (London: HMSO, 1898–1969).

Dawson, Jane E. A. *John Knox*. New Haven: Yale University Press, 2015.

Gray, John R. "The Political Theory of John Knox." *Church History 8* (June 1939).

Guy, John A. *My Heart Is My Own: The Life of Mary Queen of Scots*. London: Fourth Estate, 2009.

Henderson, G. D. *The Scots Confession, 1560*. Edinburgh: Saint Andrew Press, 1960.

Knox, John. *The History of the Reformation of Religion in Scotland*. Glasgow: Blackie, Fullarton, & Co., 1831.

———. *The Works of John Knox*. Edited by Laing David. 6 vols. Edinburgh: James Thin, 1895.

Lorimer, Peter. *John Knox and the Church of England*. London, 1875.

Marshall, Rosalind K. *John Knox*. Edinburgh: Birlinn, 2008.

Melville, J. *The Autobiography and Diary of Mr James Melville, Minister of Kilrenny in Fife*. Edited by R. Pitcairn. Edinburgh, 1842.

"The Scottish Reformation." Accessed November 26, 2016. http://www.stgilescathedral.org.uk/saint-giles-history/scottish-reformation.

Copyright and Credits

Copyright © 2016 Andy Kuo

All rights reserved. This book may not be reproduced in whole or in part, in any form without written permission from the author.

Photos are the property of the original copyright owners. They are used with permission, under the following licenses, and/or via Wikimedia Commons.
CC BY-SA 1.0: http://creativecommons.org/licenses/by-sa/1.0/
CC BY-SA 2.0: http://creativecommons.org/licenses/by-sa/2.0/
CC BY-SA 3.0: http://creativecommons.org/licenses/by-sa/3.0/
CC BY-SA 4.0: http://creativecommons.org/licenses/by-sa/4.0/

Maps except *Knox's Europe* are made available under the Open Database License: http://opendatacommons.org/licenses/odbl/1.0/. Any rights in individual contents of the database are licensed under the Database Contents License: http://opendatacommons.org/licenses/dbcl/1.0/

About the Book

John Knox, Scotland's great sixteenth-century reformer, was a man of fearless faith and unusual experiences. His faith in God turned him from a Catholic priest to a fiery Protestant preacher. His determination helped him to survive as a French galley slave, and he later served as a chaplain at King Edward VI's court in England. His belief in sharing the living Word of God led him and other English-speaking exiles in Geneva to translate the Bible into English. This Geneva Bible immediately became the most popular English Bible of its time. Knox's deep trust in God's living Word, and his charismatic preaching, boosted the morale of the Protestant movements in Scotland and eventually led to the successful establishment of Protestantism there.

This book will take you on a twofold journey: first and foremost, a journey to discover the life and faith of John Knox, a man who prevailed against difficulties and challenges because of his strong faith in God. It is also a journey following Knox's footsteps to the towns of Haddington, St Andrews, Perth, Stirling, Edinburgh, Newcastle, Berwick-upon-Tweed, Frankfurt, Dieppe, and Geneva. In each town, readers will encounter the churches, castles, and historical sites that held special significance to Knox. Maps, photos and historical background are included to help readers become acquainted with the places introduced.

www.ingramcontent.com/pod-product-compliance
Lightning Source LLC
Chambersburg PA
CBHW040329300426
44113CB00020B/2702